T0162594

REVIVE!
The Oracles of God

The Three Constants of the Christian Faith

- The Word of God
- Prayer
- Selfless Service

OZAKIEONISO CHARLIE

WESTBOW
PRESS
A DIVISION OF THOMAS NELSON

WestBow Press books may be ordered through booksellers or by contacting:

WestBow Press
A Division of Thomas Nelson
1663 Liberty Drive
Bloomington, IN 47403
www.westbowpress.com
1-(866) 928-1240

ISBN: 978-1-4497-9010-3 (sc)
ISBN: 978-1-4497-9012-7 (hc)
ISBN: 978-1-4497-9011-0 (e)

Library of Congress Control Number: 2013905962

Printed in the United States of America.

WestBow Press rev. date: 8/05/2013

Dedication

To the loving memory of my father, Vincent Charlie,
who after coming to the knowledge of God, never
ceased to pray for the salvation of his family.

To Jesus my Lord and savior the author and finisher of my faith.

Acknowledgements

This work is the result of an earnest desire for spiritual growth, revival; more of God and more of God-centred Christianity: Against the lukewarmness and just-maintain-the-status-quo mindset approach that has pervaded the body of Christ.

To the many great teachers, pastors, mentors, counselors authors etc., whose sole desire and work is to see the power of God breaking forth in a new dimension never before seen in this our dispensation, who want to see the world turned upside down for Jesus: I owe a debt of gratitude.

To the millions of believers who are genuinely looking to push the limits of revival; you inspired this work.

To my family, in-laws and friends who invested prayer, energy, their resources and interest in my life and in this work; I am very grateful and indebted.

To my beloved wife Patience Charlie, for your prayer, hard work in typing the manuscript and your valuable contributions; I appreciate you.

And most importantly, the Lord God almighty whose vineyard I seek to be through to my last breathe; I am eternally indebted for the gift of salvation and for having a divine assignment for me, personally.

CONTENTS

PREFACE

Throughout the Bible, history-making events and mind-defying acts of God are done when men step out to honor God, defend His name and/or do His will, but whether these stories are inspired by a divine burden or a message indirectly from Him (through His Word, the Holy Bible) or an answer to His direct calling, man has always been part of every work that the Lord has done on earth: And the common denominator with every one of these people that the Lord has used so mightily: is the word of God, Prayer and selfless service (The oracles of God). Abraham, for example; believed God for His word, moved across a continent to go claim His promise. Prayed to God for an heir and thereby making himself available for the service of the Lord God almighty.

In this work (Revive! The oracles of God), I want to point you to these three oracles of God, which also doubles as the three constants of our Christian faith. These oracles are consistent, dependable, ever-relevant, irreplaceable, inseparable, and sustainable with utmost potential/power —the power of faith in the word of God, prayer and selfless service (service). From putting together the complete message of salvation of God (the Holy Bible) to the election of the people of God, to the deliverance of a nation from bondage, to the parting of the Red Sea, to the conquering of the Promised Land, to the conception and the birth of the Messiah, Jesus Christ, the only begotten Son of God who had to come down as a man to show the way, He died as a man and rose as a man. All these events and every other event in history were performed by the Lord through men and women that trusted in His word, people who prayed relentlessly and who made themselves available to serve His divine purpose; and so is all future divine events: from revival, to healing the sick, to deliverance from bondage and to making ready a people for the rapture. The Bible says in Hebrews 11:21, "By faith Jacob, when he was a dying, blessed both the sons of Joseph; and worshiped, leaning upon the top of his staff." Against all odds, Jacob believed that God would bring to pass the promise of God unto Abraham.

The Word of God, whether written or the incarnate Word (Christ Jesus), is the source of all godly messages, and it has the answers to all of man's questions about God and life. The Bible stirs up godly burdens (an unction or a leading, revealing to us His divine will, convicting us of sin and preparing us for a life of righteousness and holiness) to set us apart for Himself. As it is written in John 17:17, "Sanctify them through thy truth: thy word is truth." The Word of God is the infallible source of godly messages, answers, and burdens. This is how it has been throughout all the ages. Because the Bible is the complete, inerrant Word of God, it is everything that an oracle should be. Every event in history has been instituted by the Word of God, and everything that will ever be has been declared by God. Every word recorded in scriptures must be fulfilled. Thus, the Bible is the complete message of salvation from the present until the end of the age.

When the Lord is angry with His poeple and refuses to speak to them or answer their prayers because of their sin, all they needed to do was to return to His Word. As we can see from the following scripture;

> But if from thence thou shalt seek the LORD thy GOD, thou shalt find Him, if thou seek Him with all thy heart and with all thy soul. When thou art in tribulation, and all these things are come upon thee, even in the later days, if thou turn to the LORD thy GOD, and shalt be

obedient unto His voice; (For the LORD thy GOD is a merciful GOD;) HE will not forsake thee, neither destroy thee, nor forget the covenant of thy fathers which he sware unto them. (Deuteronomy 4:29–31)

In His Word, there is the complete message of salvation. We can find all the answers and burdens to revive our relationship with Him. Whenever the people of God orders their life according to His will; then they will begin to experience again all His greatness, power, glory, victory, and majesty. The Word of God will convict you and set you apart (sanctify you) and put you on the right path with Him when you hearken to Him in obedience and believe in Him (faith). Whenever His children realizes what their shortcomings are, after they receive knowledge in righteousness (by searching the Scripture), prayer naturally follows (flows). The Bible says, "If my people, which are called by my name, shall humble themselves, and pray, and seek my face, and turn from their wicked ways; then will I hear from heaven, and will forgive their sin, and will heal their land" (2 Chronicles 7:14). Prayer is communion with God. It is available to every believer, and the Lord has promised that when we pray, He will answer. "Offer unto God thanksgiving; and pay thy vows unto the most High: And call upon me in the day of trouble: I will deliver thee, and thou shalt glorify me" (Psalm 50:14–15).

The Word of GOD also says in Jeremiah 33:3, "Call unto me, and I will answer thee, and show thee great and mighty things, which thou knowest not."

In John 14:14, the Bible says, "If ye shall ask anything in my name, I will do it." These are examples of promises that the Lord God has made regarding prayer and those who have taken Him to task on His promise of answered prayer, by actually praying hath almost, always experienced the faithfulness of God throughout all generation to the present time. For example, Isaac prayed in Genesis 25:21. "And Isaac entreated the LORD for his wife, because she was barren: and the LORD was entreated of him, and Rebecca his wife conceived." And the Bible says he was entreated of God.

With that said, prayer is nothing short of an oracle. When we pray, God sends an answer or a message. He gives us a burden that will directly meet or even surpass our petitions and requests. This is the second oracle that needs revival. Because of prayerlessness, the enemy has encroached into the church and messed us all up.

The third oracle that needs revival is you, and I will call it selfless service (absolute worship). Consider Anna or Simeon in Luke 2:25–38.

> And, behold, there was a man in Jerusalem, whose name was Simeon; and the same man was just and devout, waiting for the consolation of Israel: and the Holy Ghost was upon him. And it was revealed unto him by the Holy Ghost, that he should not see death, before he had seen the LORD's Christ. And he came by the Spirit into the temple: and when the parents brought in the child JESUS, to do for him after the custom of the law, then took he him up in his arms, and blessed GOD, and said, LORD, now lettest thou thy servant depart in peace, according to thy word: For mine eyes have seen thy salvation, which thou hast prepared before the face of all people; a light to lighten the Gentiles, and the glory of thy people Israel. And Joseph and his mother marveled at those things which were spoken of Him. And Simeon blessed them, and said unto Mary His mother, Behold, this child is set for the fall and rising again of many in Israel; and for a sign which shall be spoken against; (Yea, a sword shall pierce through thy own soul also) that the thought of many hearts may be revealed. And there was one Anna, a prophetess, the daughter of Phanuel, of the tribe of Asher: she was of a great age, and had lived with

a husband seven years from her virginity; and she was a widow of about fourscore and four years, which departed not from the temple, but served GOD with fasting and prayers night and day. And she coming in that instant gave thanks likewise unto the LORD, and spake of Him to all them that looked for redemption in Jerusalem.

Or consider Jabez in 1 Chronicles 4:9–10.

And Jabez was more honorable than his brethren: and his mother called his name Jabez, saying, Because I bare him with sorrow. And Jabez called on the GOD of Israel, oh that thou wouldest bless me indeed, and enlarge my coast, and that thine hand might be with me, and that thou wouldest keep me from evil, that it may not grieve me! And GOD granted him that which he requested.

Or think of Moses, David, or Joshua. We all have a duty to lift high the name of our Lord and Savior, Jesus, to defend and take the gospel to every corner of the universe, and to push back the enemy from our land (domain) on which he has encroached. Are you a minister of God in your church or a worker? Do you have a title or designation, or are you just an ordinary member? Either way, there is a divine purpose for you. Your name will be called out in heaven after your mission here on earth. Something very unique and personal that the Lord has put in you that He is calling out for right now. It is readily at your disposal, if only you will revive the oracle of the word and the oracle of prayer. Then the oracle of selfless service will become vivid to you. There is no limit to what you can accomplish for our Lord Jesus Christ, and we can be wiser than the ancient and have understanding more than our teachers. "I have more understanding than all my teachers: for thy testimonies are my meditation. I understand more than the ancients, because I keep thy precepts" (Psalm 119:99–100).

This is not pride. This is the provision that the Lord Himself has made for us. And no teacher should be jealous or even bitter if his or her students excel them. They should be proud. If an illiterate like Samuel Morris (read his story in the introduction) can do it, what stops you and me? The power of God is available, and there is room to be better than the ancients and your teachers. We need to take advantage of this great offer. You cannot hear this truth and remain boxed in by some man-made doctrines and denominational inadequacies. You can do muchmore than you give yourself credit for; the word of God says so; " I can do all things through Christ which strengtheneth me" – Philippians 4:13.

Do Not Limit yourself

The truth is that there is no one single denomination that gives you all that you require for a successful Christian walk from the pulpit alone., and the fact that certain denominational doctrines are unscriptural, man-made, and outright lies from the bottom of hell designed to box you in is even truer. This is why a personal quest for God and personal growth is so vital for success. Most denominations or ministries have come to their climax in the power of God and have flattened out because of the absence of the daily personal quest for God and the desire for personal growth. Church leaders hit their climaxes as soon as they begin, and the followers are following blindly. They will never be able to get anywhere. And it does not matter how big the congregation is, how good the message or music is, or how moving the congregational prayers may seem. If there is no personal desire for growth, if the individual Christian is not willing to pick up the Bible to read, study, and meditate for an hour a day, if people are not ready to bend their knees for at least an hour a day in prayer for the primary purpose of knowing His will and fulfilling His divine purpose, the church of God will continue to experience powerlessness.

The psalmist says in Psalm 42:1–11,

> As the hart panteth after the water brooks, so panted my soul after thee, O GOD. My soul thirsted for GOD, for the living GOD: when shall I appear before GOD? My tears have been my meat day and night, while they continually say unto me, where is thy GOD? When I remember these things, I pour out my soul in me; for I had gone with the multitude, I went with them to the house of GOD, with the voice of joy and praise, with a multitude that kept holyday. Why art thou cast down, O my soul? And why art thou disquieted in me? Hope thou in GOD: for I shall yet praise Him for the help of His countenance. O my GOD, my soul is cast down within me: therefore will I remember from the land of Jordan, and of the hermonites, from the hill Mizar, deep calleth unto deep at the noise of thy waterspouts: all thy waves and thy billows are gone over me. Yet the LORD will command His loving-kindness in the daytime, and in the night His song shall be with me, and my prayer unto the GOD of my life. I will say unto my rock, why has thou forgotten me? Why go I mourning because of the oppression of the enemy? As with a sword in my bones, mine enemies reproach me; while they say daily unto me, where is thy GOD? Why art thou cast down, O my soul? And why art thou disquieted in me? Hope thou in GOD: for I shall yet praise Him, who is the health of my countenance, and my GOD.

The deer long eargerly for water constantly. The deer is not like the camel or any other animal that can go without water for days or weeks at a time. The deer must drink water regularly. In the same vein, we cannot afford to stay away from the Word of God or from praying to Him or even not knowing what we should be doing for

Him. The truth is that you can afford not to pray for blessings daily, but your quest for the Lord and your desire for growth must be a daily affair.

Without a constant flow of the Word of God in and out of us, relentless praying and willingness to serve His purpose; Spiritual decay is eminent. The Word of our Lord and Savior, Jesus, puts it more rightly in Matthew 6:33. "Seek ye first the kingdom of GOD and His righteousness and all these things shall be added unto you."

Do you want to enjoy the promises of God? Then develop an insatiable appetite for the things of the kingdom of heaven through God's Word, prayer, and selfless service.

"Pant for them, long for them" (Psalm 42). If you are able to read this, you are qualified to start a revival, both personal and in the body of Christ. The Lord is calling upon you to jump out of the doctrinal box and rise above the denominational inadequacies to leap into the realm of your personal quest for God and the personal desire for growth with limitless possibilities. Any other thing is an excuse. Know this today that as a Christian believer, there is no limit to what you can accomplish for God. The key to reviving the oracles of God is reading, studying, meditating on the Word of God (i.e., personal quest for God), praying, identifying your purpose, and doing something about it (selfless service).

Let me be clear. I am not suggesting or counseling that you should leave your church or you should stop attending church services. No! These are intricate parts of your growth and service to God. In Hebrew 10:24–25, the Word of God says, "And let us consider one another to provoke unto love and to good works. Not forsaking the assembly of ourselves together, as the manner of some is: but exhorting one another: and so much the more, as ye see the day approaching." Rather, I am suggesting that you develop a personal desire for growth and a deep personal longing for God where you will not be boxed in by man-made doctrines and denominational inadequacies.

What are you doing for God right now? Are you counting tithes and offerings of the church? That is good, but my question is this: Is that all you can do for all that Christ has done for you? Do you sing in the choir? That's noble work! Are you an usher? Great! Are you a prayer warrior or an intercessor? Excellent! But this is what God desire of you: that you find your divine purpose and fulfill it. God is willing to baptize you with His power so that what you do will carry the authority of heaven for greater harvests and results. Do not be like those that the Bible describes in; 2 Timothy 3:5. "Having the form of godliness, but denying the power thereof: from such turn away."

It is never too late as God's Word says in Hebrew 3:7–17.

> Ever learning and never able to come to the knowledge of the truth. Now as James and Jambres withstood Moses, so do these also resist the truth: men of corrupt minds reprobates concerning the faith. But they shall proceed no further: for their folly shall be manifest unto all men, as theirs was, but thou hast fully known my doctrine, manner of life, purpose, faith, longsuffering, charity, patience. Persecutions, affliction, which came unto me at Antioch, at Iconium, at Lystra: what persecutions I endured: but out of them all, the LORD delivered me. Yea and all that will live godly in Christ JESUS shall suffer persecution, but evil men and seducers shall wax worse and worse, deceiving, and being deceived. But continue thou in the things which thou hast learned and hast been assured of, knowing of whom thou hast learned them. And that from a child thou hast known the Holy scriptures, which are able to make thee wise unto salvation through faith which is in Christ JESUS. All scripture is given by inspiration of GOD, and is profitable for doctrine, for reproof, for correction, for instruction in righteousness: That the man of GOD may be perfect, thoroughly furnished unto all good works.

INTRODUCTION

Therefore they say unto GOD, depart from us; for we desire not the knowledge of thy ways. What is the Almighty that we should serve Him? And what profit should we have, if we pray unto Him?
—Job 21:14–15

The Bible refer to those who reject the knowledge of God, prayer, and service of the Lord God Almighty as the "wicked." Far too many Christians are content with warming the pews on Sunday. Others are interested in being seen as "working" for God rather than finding personal time of reading, studying, and meditating on the Word of God, times of personal praying and giving oneself completely to the service of the Lord (selfless service).

In the late nineteenth century, a young African prince by the name of Samuel Morris was used so mightily of God at the Taylor University in Fort Wayne, Indiana. His story typified and highlighted the oracles of God that we want to discuss in the chapters of this book. All are impressed by his earnest desire to know God better, his natural appetite for praying at all times, and his natural flare to serve others and bring the light of God to every dark corner of the people he comes in contact with so that they may be impacted by His unfailing love. His story reveals in all practical terms the oracle of God's Word, the oracle of prayer, and the oracle of selfless service.

Prince Kaboo, as he was first known, was born to be the king of a

1

small clan in the primitive jungles of Liberia in West Africa. His clan was vulnerable to another much bigger and stronger clan. This bigger clan invaded them at will, robbed them of their possessions, and captured or killed their young men at will. They were always living in fear, not knowing when the next attack would come. In one such invasion, Prince Kaboo was captured by the rival clan and used as a pawn to force his father to pay ransom to the king of the rival clan before he would be released. As he was led away with his hands tied behind his back, his father tried to assure him that everything would be okay and that he would pay whatever the rival king requested for his son's freedom and bring him back home. The payment was expected by the next new moon. Prince Kaboo's father gathered all that he could and brought the ransom to the king for his son to be released, but the rival king condemned it and said it was too small. By the following new moon, he brought yet more gifts for the ransom of his son, but it seemed like no matter what he brought, the king of the rival clan would never be satisfied. New moon after new moon, he came with more gifts and got the same result every time, and each time he came, his gifts got the king angrier. He would order his men to beat and torture Prince Kaboo. And after so many attempts with gifts to buy back the prince had failed, King Kaboo decided to give his little daughter, Prince Kaboo's younger sister, for the ransom of his son. The rival king felt even more insulted than ever before. He called the daughter worthless. And when prince Kaboo's father left this time, the rival king was determined to kill Prince Kaboo. He ordered that his men dig a pit and bury Prince Kaboo up to his neck and pour honey over his head to attract the most poisonous ants and then leave him to die. While they were digging the pit, the prince was hanging on a tree, both his hands and feet tied. He had been so badly beaten that he was drifting in and out of consciousness. But when the men finish digging the grave and were threatening to bury him in it, a light suddenly flashed from heaven, a light that blinded his captors and their king momentarily. The strings that they had used to tie up the prince fell off from his hands and feet, and Prince Kaboo heard a voice say, "Run! Run!" He did not know where he got the strength, but he started to run. He ran; despite the days he had slept tied to tree trunks and without food. And for weeks, he ran, not knowing where he was running to, hiding from people when he noticed them so that they would not recapture him for a reward. He ate only fruits and plant roots. He traveled long and far until he stumbled upon the edge of a coffee plantation. He heard people singing. He carefully drew closer and saw a boy about his age. He decided to approach this boy. Fortunately, this boy was from the same clan as he was and recognized the prince. The boy was surprised to see his prince because Prince Kaboo was scarred all over and emaciated from the beatings, starvation, and the terribly long journey through the wilderness. Then this boy from his village decided to take the prince in and bring him to the owners of the plantation, who were his employer; who helped take care of him and nurse him back to good health. When the prince got well, the prince's tribe boy found him work on the coffee farm. The owners of the farm were slaves who had returned from America after the abolition of the slave trade, and they were also Christians.

The boy from his native land told him about the living God, and Prince Kaboo soon expressed interest in becoming a Christian. He accepted Jesus Christ into his life and learned to pray (how to talk to his heavenly Father, as he called it). When he heard the story about how the apostle Paul was converted, he recognized the light that had flashed on the night of his escape and the voice that had also told him to run. He knew that it had been this God that had delivered him that night from the cruel king. Prince Kaboo learned some English, and the more he heard the Word of God, the more he wanted it. He was then baptized, and when he learned how to pray, he was always asking God for everything he needed through prayer. He prayed for everything he wanted and realized that almost, everything he prayed for came to pass. After the baptism, his name was changed from

Prince Kaboo to Samuel Morris. Samuel Morris called the Lord his Father and Jesus his brother. He was overwhelmed with joy when he came to the knowledge of this God that loved him so much and saved him from the evil king, something his earthly father could not do. He was determined to learn more about his heavenly Father. He was always looking for new opportunities to learn more of the Lord.

One day, he heard about the power and work of the Holy Ghost in the life of believers. He wanted the Holy Ghost so badly, and his teachers told him that for him to receive the Holy Ghost, he needed to go to America and visit Stephen Meritt. That man would be the one to help the prince receive the Holy Ghost. Samuel Morris made up his mind there and then, to go to America to meet Stephen Meritt. The missionary that told him about the Holy Ghost and Stephen Meritt told him that it would cost him one hundred dollars to go to America. Samuel Morris said that his father would provide. He prayed to God to bring him to America so that he could meet Stephen Meritt and receive the Holy Ghost. He went to Monrovia, the capital of Liberia, and at the harbor, he learned that there was an American ship there that would be living for the United States soon. Samuel Morris was overjoyed. Because he didn't have any money, he prayed that God would take him to America in the ship. An opportunity came when he saw the captain of the ship coming to shore with his crew. He waited for the captain, and when the captain came, Samuel told him that he wanted to go to America with him on his ship. The captain looked at him. The boy was so tattered, and he wasn't wearing good clothing. The captain was so mad that he kicked Samuel Morris hard, but that did not deter the young boy. Samuel Morris approached the captain again when he was going back to the ship, and the prince pleaded with him. Samuel said he would work hard for the captain in exchange for his passage to America. The captain thought he needed someone anyway, to fill a role, because one of his regular staff had eloped with a woman and he was short of a crew. And so Sammy (as he was fondly called later on by all the crew) got a job on the ship. His life on that ship was a nightmare. He was beaten, and he was verbally abused every day. On one occasion, the captain hit him so hard that the prince was knocked unconscious. The following day when he regained consciousness, he held no grudges against the captain. He continued with his services as if nothing had ever happened. God would soon turn things around for Sammy. He always prayed and sang hymns he had memorized.

When they came to a certain island, the crew was attacked by a band of pirates. The attack was so daring that some of the crew members were killed, and a lot of their attackers were also slain. While the attack was happening, the captain, who was always drunk and who had never liked Sammy, called him up and asked him to start praying for their deliverance. Sammy obliged. He fell on his knees and prayed for the deliverance of their ship and crew, and God answered. At the end of it all, the ship was delivered. They had lost a few men, and some had been wounded; however, the majority of the crew came out unscathed. Sammy became the nurse for the wounded, and he also prayed for them. The captain instituted prayer meetings on board the ship every day, and Sammy led them. Everyone came to love him, and they were all filled with admiration for him. They all gave their hearts to Jesus before they arrived at New York City, the destination of the ship. Sammy, who had come on board with only a pieces of tattered clothe on his back, now had a box filled with clothing, a gift from the captain and crew members.

In New York, Samuel Morris met a homeless black man and asked him to take him to Stephen Meritt. The prince knew that the odds of anybody knowing Stephen Meritt in such a big city were beyond impossible, but as destiny would have it, this homeless man has been a regular beneficiary at the mission house that was owned by Stephen Meritt. Right away, the homeless man said, "I will take you to Stephen Meritt, but it will cost you a dollar."

Sammy said, "I will pay." He didn't have a penny on him, but he trusted that God would take care of his expenses now that He has brought him to New York City to meet Stephen Meritt. When they got to Stephen Meritt, he was just locking his door to leave the office for an appointment. His guide pointed to Stephen Meritt and said, "That's him."

Sammy went to Stephen Meritt and said, "I come from Africa to you so you can teach me about the Holy Ghost."

Stephen Meritt asked him if he had a letter from the missionary that sent him, and Samuel said that he didn't have a letter. He told him that he could not wait for such a letter because it was urgent and that he needed to receive the Holy Ghost. But Stephen Meritt had to go, so he directed him to the mission house where the meals were being served. And then as he was about to move, his guide demanded, "Where is my dollar?"

Sammy turned to Stephen Meritt and said, "You have to give this man a dollar." Luckily, Stephen Meritt gladly paid. After they ate at the mission house, everybody waited for a prayer meeting. A young man led the meeting, and when he finished, Sammy stepped to the podium and told them how God had delivered him from his captors in the jungles of Liberia a few years back and how God had brought him miraculously to America to see Stephen Meritt. Then he knelt on the altar and prayed. The people were so moved after his testimony that everybody in the room came forward and knelt around him, weeping profusely and praying at the same time. At that moment, Stephen Meritt came in from his appointment, and he beheld the sight of everyone weeping and praying for the salvation of the Lord. This was just the beginning of a mighty move of God through this uneducated African boy, and Stephen Meritt knew that God would use this man to touch many lives and most importantly, the lives of those who were supposed to teach him about God and the Holy Ghost. There began a series of mighty move of God through Samuel Morris in so many places he went and everybody he met. Mrs. Merit did not like the fact that Sammy, an African boy was in their house and that he was so shabbily clothed. She did not think he belonged with them. Friends of Stephen Meritt felt insulted to have Sammy seat in the same carriage with them. On one occasion Stephen Merittt ask Sammy to accompany him to a funeral service, there those that were present witness his praying anointing, when he was called upon to pray at that service. Sammy's prayer moved many to repentance and to rededicate their lives to God and the move of God was very apparent. He was divinely accepted into Taylor University without even possessing the most basic skills of reading or writing. However, he impacted the university daily and the neighboring community at large with his simple faith and relentless praying and his zeal to serve. It is reported that Sammy had an encounter with a renowned atheist that gave his heart to God after Sammy prayed for him and he became a believer. Revival broke out in every church he visited. People felt the anointing of God whenever he spoke or prayed. Through him, Taylor University was taken from the fringe of bankruptcy and raised ten thousand dollars for a bigger property. Samuel Morris had done all this within two years after he had arrived in America at the young age of twenty. Before his death, he had impacted so many lives, and he continues to impact so many today who read his story. He has inspired people and moved them to seek God through the knowledge of His Word, relentless praying, and the desire to share the realization of God's love with the world.

Samuel Morris wanted to know God and the power of His might better. He was passionate to know everything he could and give everything as well (if that was a possibility). Meanwhile, in the quest for more of the Lord, he was increasing and abounding in His power. Through his insatiable appetite for the Word of God, relentless praying, and the desire for selfless service, he became an inspiration to even his teachers and the elders of the day.

As the Bible says in Matthew 6:33, "But seek ye first the kingdom of GOD and His righteousness, and all these things shall be added unto you."

The oracle of the Word of God, the oracle of prayer, and the oracle of selfless service are the most powerful and easily accessible sources for the Lord God Almighty and His glory. How can we seek the kingdom of God and all His righteousness? We can achieve this through increasing our knowledge of Him, relentless praying, and the burning desire to share His light and love (selfless service) with this wicked world that so desperately needs His light and His unfailing love.

Before Sammy died, he did so much without any education. He has left powerful footprints that cannot be washed away. We can all follow his footprints, and they will lead us all to the same experience of the raw and undiluted power of God, a power that will impact our communities, cities, states, nations, and the world. Does the church today need a revival? Yes! If we all agree on this, then pick up your Bible and start reading, studying, and meditating on the Word of God. Prayerfully ask Him to give you the hunger for His knowledge and His anointing of the Holy Ghost. Pray Psalm 119:18. "Open thou mine eyes, that I may behold wondrous things out of thy law." And begin to live a life of selfless service. Then revival will break forth, not only in your life but also in your church and in the body of Christ as a whole.

Let us stop buying into the suggestions of the Devil that the Bible is difficult to understand, that that knowledge is given only to a gifted few to understand and interpret for the rest of us. Do not give in to the argument that the Word of God contradicts itself and cannot be the basis for truth. Do not sell out to the idea that as long as you live a good life and do good things, the Bible does not matter. After all, isn't that the general idea of the Bible, namely to be good and do good unto others? However, only in the Bible can you perfect the act of being good. Consider this obvious but deep spiritual truth. The Holy Bible is an oracle of God! Prayer is also an oracle. If prayer is talking to God and you can believe it; there you are before GOD talking to Him and knowing that He hears you and will answer: that is a powerful oracle of God. Jesus talked about the plenteous harvest referring to those that need to be won over into the kingdom of God and how the laborers are few referring to the need of more workers for the kingdom of God (Matthew 9: 36-38). Will you want to be used of God mightily to rein in the harvest? God will do His work through people, and the idea that you can be used by Him to reach the unreached, touch those who need His touch, inspire those whose hope are fading, minister healing to the sick, deliverance to those in bondage, blessings, and ultimately salvation to the lost, is the most practical unity with God. Selfless service is an oracle of God.

Revive!!! The oracle of God.

Chapter 1

WHAT IS AN ORACLE?

For my people have committed two evils; they have forsaken
me the fountain of living waters, and hewed them out
cisterns, broken cisterns, that can hold no water.
—Jeremiah 2:13

Let us search and try our ways, and turn again to the LORD, Let
us lift up our heart with our hands unto God in the heavens.
—Lamentations 3:40–41

So shall my word be that goeth forth out of my mouth: it shall
not return unto me void, but it shall accomplish that which I
please, and it shall prosper in the thing whereto I sent it.
—Isaiah 55:11

I have sworn by myself, the word is gone out of my
mouth in righteousness, and shall not return, that unto
me every knee shall bow, every tongue shall swear.
—Isaiah 45:23

Remember the former things of old: for I am GOD, and there
is none else; I am GOD, and there is none like me.
—Isaiah 46:9–11

Heaven and earth shall pass away, but my words shall not pass away.
—Matthew 24:35

In simple terms, an oracle is a place, person, or means through which one receives divine messages, answers, or burdens (unctions, leadings or burning desire from the Lord: to be somewhere with His message, or do something for His glory, or give a helping hand to someone in need, etc.).

When King Josiah was read to from the book of the Law that was found during the renovation works that he had ordered in the temple of God, it marked one of the greatest revivals in the history of the nation of Israel. 2 Chronicles 34:14–21 says,

> And when they brought out the money that was brought into the house of the LORD, Hilkiah the priest found a book of the law of the LORD given by Moses. And Hilkiah answered and said to Shaphan the scribe, I have found the book of the law in the house of the LORD. And Hilkiah delivered the book to Shaphan. And Shaphan carried the book to the king, and brought the king word back again, saying, All that was committed to thy servants, they do it. And they have gathered together the money that was found in the house of the LORD, and have delivered it into the hand of the overseers, and to the hand of the workmen. Then Shaphan the scribe told the king, saying, Hilkiah the priest hath given me a book. And Shaphan read it before the king. And it came to pass, when the king had heard the words of the law, that he rent his clothes. And the king commanded Hilkih, and Ahikam the son of Shaphan, and Abdon the son of Micah, and Shaphan the scribe, and Asaiah a servant of the king's, saying. Go, inquire of the LORD for me, and for them that are left in Israel and in Judah, concerning the words of the book that is found: for great is the wrath of the LORD that is poured out upon us, because our fathers have not kept the word of the LORD, to do after all that is written in this book.

When he heard from the book of the Law, King Josiah knew that Israel (Judah) had sinned greatly against God and had to seek a way to return to Him. The people had to learn how to revive their relationship (covenant) with God. During the return from exile, the leader who led the spiritual revival of the devastated nation of Israel and the rebuilding of the temple was described as follows in Ezra 7:6–10:

> This Ezra went up from Babylon; and he was a ready scribe in the law of Moses, which the LORD GOD of Israel had given: and the king granted him all his request, according to the hand of the LORD his GOD upon him. And there went up some of the children of Israel, and of the priest of the levites, and the singers, and the porters, and the Nethinims, unto Jerusalem, in the seventh year of Artaxerxes the king. And he came to Jerusalem in the fifth month, which was in the seventh year of the king. For upon the first day of the first month began he to go up from Babylon and on the first day of the fifth month came he to Jerusalem, according to the good hand of his GOD upon him. For Ezra had prepared his heart to seek the law of the LORD, and to do it, and to teach in Israel statutes and judgments.

These two individuals, who were set apart by centuries, received divine burdens and answers through the knowledge and revelation of the law of God. Because of this, the hand of the Lord was revealed through them. Ezra 7:6 says, "This Ezra went up from Babylon; and he was a ready scribe in the law of Moses, which the LORD GOD of Israel had given: and the king granted him all his request, according to the hand of the LORD his GOD upon him." Whenever people of God—whether individually or collectively—decide to study the Bible, seek understanding, and live according to the Word of God, the hand of God is revealed through them. Every revival since biblical times to the present has been rooted in the Word of God, including the Welch Revival, the Azuza Street Revival, or the Solomon Island Revival.

The Word of God contains power to deliver the complete message of salvation and eternity, answer every question about life and the nature and character of God, and stir up burdens in the hearts of people against sin. It speaks about what the Lord desires of His people at all times—even on specific issues concerning the believer, his or her immediate environment, or even the future. Hebrews 4:12 says, "For the word of GOD is quick and powerful, and sharper than any two-edged sword piercing even to the dividing asunder of soul and spirit, and of the joints and marrow, and is a discerner of the thoughts and intents of the heart."

The fact that Scripture carries an ever-relevant message that cuts across all generations for all humankind, that it has answers to every life question, need, or desire, and that it reveals the helpless state of humanity without its maker and our sinful nature cannot be overemphasized. God's Word has the power to deliver relevant divine messages, answer life questions, and stir up divine burdens for a better working relationship with God. Hence, it can nurture to a state of perfection. Consider the following quotations:

> So shall my word be that goeth out of my mouth: it shall not return unto me void, but it shall accomplish that which I please, and it shall prosper in the thing whereto I send it. (Isaiah 55:11)

> Remember the former things of old: for I am GOD, and there is none else; I am GOD and there is none like me. Declaring the end from the beginning, and from ancient times the things that are not yet done, saying, My counsel shall stand, and I will do all my pleasure. Calling a ravenous bird from the east, the man that executeth my counsel from a far country: yea, I have spoken it, I will

also bring it to pass; I have purposed it, I will also do it. (Isaiah 46:9–11)

Heaven and earth shall pass away, but my word shall not pass away. (Matthew 24:35)

The power in the Word of God can only be made to work when the individual believer decides to understand and live according to it.

Hear what the Psalmist says in Psalm 119:89-96. "For ever, O LORD, thy word is settled in heaven.

Thy faithfulness is unto all generations: thou hast established the earth, and it abideth.

They continue this day according to thine ordinances: for all are thy servants.

Unless thy law had been my delights, I should then have perished in mine affliction.

I will never forget thy precepts: for with them thou hast quickened me.

I am thine, save me: for I have sought thy precepts.

The wicked have waited for me to destroy me: but I will consider thy testimonies.

I have seen an end of all perfection: but thy commandment is exceeding broad.

The bible is not just a holy book it is the word of God.

Isaac prayed to the Lord for his wife, Rebecca, because she was barren. "And Isaac entreated the LORD for his wife, because she was barren: and the LORD was entreated of him, and Rebecca his wife conceived" (Genesis 25:21). Hannah prayed to the Lord God of

Israel when there was nobody to turn to. Her mate taunted her and called her names.

> So Hannah rose up after they had eaten in Shiloh, and after they had drunk. Now Eli the priest sat upon a seat by a post of the temple of the LORD. And she was in bitterness of soul, and prayed unto the LORD, and wept sore. And she vowed a vow, and said, O LORD of Hosts, if thou wilt indeed look on the affliction of thine handmaid, and remember me, and not forget thine handmaid, but wilt give unto thine handmaid a man child, then I will give him unto the LORD all the days of his life, and there shall no razor come upon his head. And it came to pass, as she continue praying before the LORD, that Eli marked her mouth. Now Hannah, she spake in her heart; only her lips moved, but her voice was not heard: therefore Eli thought she had been drunken. And Eli said unto her, how long wilt thou be drunken? Put away thy wine from thee. And Hannah answered and said, No, my LORD, I am a woman of a sorrowful spirit: I have drunk neither wine nor strong drink, but have poured out my soul before the LORD. Count not thine handmaid for a daughter of Belial: for out of the abundance of my complaint and grief have I spoken hitherto. Then Eli answered and said, Go in peace: and the GOD of Israel grant thy petition that thou hast asked of Him. And she said, Let thine handmaid find grace in thy sight. So the woman went her way, and did eat, and her countenance was no more sad. And they rose up in the morning early, and worshiped before the LORD, and returned, and came to their house in Ramah: and Elkanah knew Hannah his wife; and the LORD remembered her. (Isaiah 1:9–19)

The apostles prayed in Acts 4:13–30.

Now when they saw the boldness of Peter and John, and perceived that they were unlearned and ignorant men, they marveled; and they took knowledge of them, that they had been with Jesus. And beholding the man which was healed standing with them, they could say nothing against it. But when they had commanded them to go aside out of the council, they conferred among themselves, Saying, what shall we do to these men? For that indeed a notable miracle hath been done by them is manifest to all men that dwell in Jerusalem; and we cannot deny it. But that it spread no further among the people, let us straitly threaten them that they speak henceforth to no man in this name. And they called them, and commanded them not to speak at all nor teach in the name of Jesus. But Peter and John answered and said unto them, whether it be right in the sight of GOD to hearken unto you more than unto GOD, judge ye. For we cannot but speak the things which we have seen and heard. So when they had further threaten them, they let them go, finding nothing how they might punish them, because of the people: for all men glorified GOD for that which was done. For the man was above forty years old, on whom this miracle of healing was showed. And being let go, they went to their own company, and reported all that the chief priests and elders had said unto them. And when they heard that, they lifted up their voice to GOD with one accord, and said, LORD, thou art GOD, which hast made heaven, and earth, and the sea, and all that in them is: Who by the mouth of thy servant David hast said, why did the heathen rage, and the people imagine vain things? The kings of the earth stood up, and the rulers were gathered together against the Lord, and against His Christ. For of a truth against thy Holy child Jesus, whom thou hast anointed, both Herod, and Pontius Pilate, with the gentiles, and the people of Israel, were gathered together, For to do whatsoever thy hand and thy counsel determine before to be done. And now, Lord, behold their threatening: and grant unto thy servants, that with all boldness they may speak thy word, by stretching forth thine hand to heal, and that signs and wonders may be done by the name of thy holy child Jesus.

Whenever an individual or group of individuals have prayed genuinely, whether individually or collectively, God has always responded in three ways. He would send a message, give an answer, or give a burden to those who prayed. Prayer is the next thing to God. It is the closest and readily available access to God. It is the most powerful cord of our relationship with God. Prayer is the only means available to man to readily access the greatness, power, glory, victory, and majesty of the Almighty. John 14:14." If ye shall ask any thing in my name, I will do it. Please note prayer is not just talking to God, it is invoking His will.

Thirdly, whenever a group of people realizes the will of God through scriptural revelations or otherwise and step out with all their hearts to do His will, God releases His power and favor through those people. God gives divine burden to willing hearts, and when they act on that burden, He provides the answer (solution) that is needed or reveals a message that will clearly declare the heart of God (His will). In the battle between David and Goliath in 1 Samuel 17:23–31, the Bible says,

And as he talked with them, behold , there came up the champion, the Philistine of Gath, Goliath by name, out of the armies of the Philistine, and spake according to the same words: and David heard them. And all the men of Israel, when they saw the man, fled from him, and were sore afraid. And the men of Israel said, have you seen this man that is come up? Surely to defy Israel is he come up: and it shall be, the man who killeth him, the king will enrich him with great riches, and will give him his daughter, and make his father's house free in Israel. And David spake to the men who stood by him, saying, what shall be done to the man that killeth this Philistine, and taketh away the reproach from Israel? For who is this uncircumcised Philistine, that he should defy the armies of the living GOD? And the people answered him after this manner, saying, So shall it be done to the man that killeth him. And Eliab his eldest brother heard when he spake unto the men; and Eliab anger was kindled against David, and he said, why camest thou hither? And with whom hast thou left those few sheep in the wilderness? I know thy pride, and the nauhgtiness of thine heart; for thou art come down that thou mightiest see the battle. And David said, what have I now done? Is there not a cause? And he turn from him toward another, and spake after the same manner: and the people answered him again after the former manner. And when the words was heard which David spake, they rehearsed them before Saul: and he sent for him.

This is a clear case of a time when a man understood what was needful for the moment to deliver the children of Israel, the people called God's elect, His chosen people, from the reproach of Goliath. This is a clear case of a divine burden upon the boy David who was so moved to step out to defend the name of the Lord God of Israel. Lets highlight some of his responses in the discussions leading to the battle with Goliath: 1Samuel 17:26,29 and 36 " And David spake to the men that stood by him, saying, What shall be done to the man that killeth this Philistine, and taketh away the reproach from Israel? for who is this uncircumcised Philistine, that he should defy the armies of the living God? 29 And David said,

What have I now done? Is there not a cause? 36 Thy servant slew both the lion and the bear: and this uncircumcised Philistine shall be as one of them, seeing he hath defied the armies of the living God. This would ultimately determine who the real God was—the gods of the Philistines or the God of Israel, the maker of heaven and earth. The third oracle I am going to discuss in the pages of this book is selfless service or simply service (absolute worship). For the purpose of this book, I will call this oracle "selfless service." Every great thing that God has ever done in the history of the world has been done through a physical man. Whenever any people make themselves available to be used by God and recognize what is needful, God will reveal Himself through such people. He can stir up a burden or give a message, and/or grant an answer or solution as necessary. Whenever a believer steps out and recognizes what is needful and says to the Lord, "Here I am. Send me," He has always been revealed through such individuals. People like Abraham, Moses, Joshua, Joseph, David, Elijah, and Elisha were all great oracles with divine powers because they stepped out where others would not dare to wink or blink. The burden to serve others according to the will of the Lord is what revives the image of God in us. In this way, we can attain states of divine power and divine ability that we could never acquire otherwise.

In the parable of the Good Samaritan, the Lord Jesus Christ teaches us a great lesson in selfless service in addition to being a good neighbor.

> And, behold, a certain lawyer stood up, and tempted Him, saying, Master, what shall I do to inherit eternal life? He said unto him, what is written in the law? How readest thou? And he answering said. Thou shalt love the LORD thy GOD with all thy heart, and with all thy soul, and with all thy strength, and with all thy mind; and thy neighbor as thyself. And He said unto him, thou hast answered right: this do, and thou shalt live. But he,

willing to justify himself, said unto JESUS, and who is my neighbor? And JESUS answering said, A certain man went down from Jerusalem to Jericho, and fell among thieves, which stripped him of his raiment, and wounded him, and departed, leaving him half dead. And by chance there came down a certain priest that way: and when he saw him, he passed by on the other side. And likewise a levite, when he was at the place, came and looked on him, and passed by on the other side. But a certain Samaritan, as he journeyed, came where he was: and when he saw him, he had compassion on him. And went to him, and bound up his wounds, pouring in oil and wine, and set him on his own beast, and brought him to an inn, and took care of him. And on the morrow when he departed, he took out two pence, and gave them to the host, and said unto him, take care of him; and whatsoever thou spendest more, when I come again, I will repay thee. Which now of these three, thiniest thou, was neighbor unto him that fell among the thieves? And he said, he that showeth mercy on him, then said JESUS unto him, Go, and do likewise. (Luke 10:25–37)

Here, the supposed keepers of the oracles of God, a priest and a Levite, came and saw the half-dead victim, and they passed on the other side. Maybe they were afraid of what it might cost them to help, or maybe they were afraid that the man might die while they are trying to help, given how bad the situation was; however, the Good Samaritan saw the same victim, rolled up his sleeves, picked up the dying man, put him on his donkey, took him to an inn, paid for his medical bills, and promised to come back to make up for any additional costs for the man's healing. And as a result, a man who could not help himself was touched mightily by God through another. Whatever you are willing to do unto the glory of God will cause all that He is to flow through you. That is what will make you His mouthpiece, bring about divine answers, or stir up a divine burden in you.

Meanwhile, will you take a giant leap of faith right now, right where you are and put what you have read so far into action by doing the following? For all practical purposes, I want you to confess these verses of scriptures and pray the prayer points following each of them, for at least ten minutes:

1. Scriptural confession: "Open thou mine eyes, that I may behold wondrous things out of thy law" (Psalm 119:18).

    Prayer point: Oh, Lord, grant me knowledge and understanding of your Word as I read, study, and meditate on the Holy Bible in the name of Jesus.

2. Scriptural confession: "Call unto me; and I will answer thee, and show thee great and mighty things, which thou knowest not" (Jeremiah 33:3).

    Prayer Point: Oh, Lord, demonstrate your prayer answering power in my life in the mighty name of Jesus.

3. Scriptural confession: "I can do all things through Christ which strengtheneth me" (Philippians 4:13).

    Prayer Point: Oh, Lord, my God, give me a burden that will start a Holy Ghost revival in me, my home, my church, and my environment in Jesus' name.

You may return to these scriptural confessions and prayer points in the next two days. You can spend thirty minutes on each prayer point on the second day and one whole hour on each prayer point during the third day.

Please perform this activity sincerely if you want a change and wait on the Lord with all your heart. He will answer you.

The Word of God, prayer, and selfless service (absolute worship) are the three constants of our Christian faith. They have been the rallying point for every great revival that has ever been and will ever be. Even today, they have the ultimate potential to transform the body of Christ and become the source of not only divine power but also divine messages, answers, and burdens for our everyday Christian living and exploits. Christians need to return to personal Bible reading, study, and meditation on the Word of God. As the Word of God says in John 8:32, "And ye shall know the truth, and the truth shall set you free." Consider also John 17:17: "Sanctify them through thy truth: thy word is truth." These scriptures should be motivations for us to search the word of God daily. As the Bible puts it in Joshua 1:8, "This book of the law shall not depart out thy mouth; but thou shalt meditate therein day and night, that thou mayest observe to do according to all that is written therein: for then thou shalt make thy way prosperous, and then thou shalt have good success."

This is the first oracle. When your life is rich in God's Word, the second (prayer) and the third (selfless service) oracles are only so natural. Church attendance is good. The community spirit is excellent. Group activities and organizational expertise are also nice. However, when these becomes the only things that believers do instead of investing in personal time spent on the Word of God, personal prayer, and daring to step out where others are afraid to, all for the glory of God, we become shortchanged and grossly inadequate in our spiritual work. If believers will not limit themselves any longer and will desire more knowledge of Him and will develop the habit of talking to Him about everything in prayer, believing in His promise to answer, and daring to do whatever His leading will be, God will be real. His presence, His power, and His glory will be ever-real, even in this our dispensation. These oracles, today more than at any other time, will cause the Holy Ghost to move in a mighty way, both within individuals and corporately in the church of God. These three oracles are ever-relevant, irreplaceable, accessible to all (within the reach of all), and sustainable with the utmost potential/power.

May I remind us that the Lord Jesus Himself, who is the incarnate Word, lived by the Word while he lived among us. Remember, service is not just a duty, but it is revealing God in you through you. He prayed relentlessly day and night, and He was on earth to serve us. If we are not following these examples of Christ, then I do not know whose we are following.

Revive the oracles of God!

Chapter 2

THE ORACLE OF THE WORD

*This book of the law shall not depart out of thy mouth; but thou
shalt meditate therein day and night, that thou mayest observe
to do according to all that is written therein: for then thou shalt
make thy way prosperous, and then thou shalt have good success.*
—Joshua 1:8.

*When thou goest, it shall lead thee; when thou sleepest, it shall
keep thee; and when thou awakest, it shall talk with thee.*
—Proverbs 6:22

*Open thou mine eyes, that I may behold
wondrous things out of thy law.*
—Psalm 119:18

*Thy word is true from the beginning: and every one
of thy righteous judgments endureth for ever.*
—Psalm 119:160.

*For the word of God is quick, and powerful, and sharper
than any two edged sword, piercing even to the dividing
asunder of soul and spirit, and of the joints and marrow, and
is a discerner of the thoughts and intents of the heart.*
—Hebrews 4:12

The most powerful passage in all Scripture is in Number 23:19. "God is not a man, that he should lie; neither the son of man, that he should repent: hath he said, and shall he not do it? or hath he spoken, and shall he not make it good?"

This means that God is truth and that God cannot lie. His immutability is stated clearly here. He cannot change. These are His two strongest characteristics. All He says is the truth, and He does not change. Therefore, His Word is the truth, and because He does not change, He eternally does what He says and makes good on everything He hath spoken. Hence, God's Word is truth. There is no lie in it. It will not fail. He does what He says. What He said a thousand years ago is true today. His bidding will be done. Because He does not change, He will not repent. His power does not diminish with time. Neither does the truth change. The truth can never become a lie.

This fusion of these two most powerful forces, namely the truth and the immutable nature of the Lord God Almighty, is what makes His Word an oracle. As it is written: "God is not a man that he should lie, neither the son of man, that he should repent hath He said, and shall he not do it? Or hath he spoken, and shall he not make it good? – Numbers 23:19. He will make it good. Whatsoever GOD hath said is the truth and the test for every truth is in its ability to stand against every contrary claims and the strength to remain true is in God's immutability." Thus, the Word of God is a living oracle because everything He says will happen for all eternity. Is it His commandments for our everyday living, His call for us to return to Him from where we have falling, the promise of His salvation from the thief, killer, and the destroyer (the enemy) or eternal life with Him in His kingdom or the condemnation of His enemies to eternity in the lake of unquenchable fire? Every word in scriptures will be fulfilled. The Lord will make good every of His promise. Isaiah puts it more clearly in Isaiah 55:11. "So shall my word be that goeth forth out of my mouth: it shall not return unto me void, but it shall accomplish that which I please, and it shall prosper in the thing whereto I sent it." The Psalmist put is simply: "For ever, O Lord, thy word is settled in heaven." –Psalm 119:89

There's an open but powerful secret in the Word of God. Every student of the Bible can pick it up readily. It is how we can draw from the power of our God daily and constantly, so that we can come to a point where His power not only works in us, but also flows from us and infects our environment and the people we come in contact with, whether personally or remotely. This is so evident in the way that the Lord God announced the second king of Israel that would take over from King Saul, who had become a disappointment to God. "But now thy kingdom shall not continue: the LORD hath sought Him a man after His own heart, and the LORD hath commanded him to be captain over his people, because thou hast not kept that which the Lord commanded thee." (1 Samuel 13:14). From this scripture, we can conclude that David was not created a king. Neither was he born one. However, by virtue of his fear of God, his love, and his willingness to do the Lord's will, he was endeared to God's heart. An overview of David's life will tell us how much he loved the Law of the Lord.

> The law of the LORD is perfect, converting the soul: the testimony of the LORD is sure, making wise the simple. The statutes of the LORD are right, rejoicing the heart: the commandment of the LORD is pure, enlightening the eyes. The fear of the LORD is clean, enduring for ever: the judgments of the LORD are true and righteous altogether. More to be desired are they than gold, yea, than much fine gold: sweeter also than honey and the honeycomb. Moreover by them is thy servant warned: and in keeping of them there is great reward. Who can understand his errors? cleanse thou me from secret faults. Keep back thy servant also from presumptuous sins; let them not have dominion over me: then shall I be upright, and I shall be innocent from the great transgression. Let the words of

> my mouth, and the meditation of my heart, be acceptable
> in thy sight, O Lord, my strength, and my redeemer.
> (Psalm 19:7–14)

His entire life was guided by the Law of the Lord, and his greatest desire was to obey the commandment of the Lord. Consider the words in Psalm 119:97–104.

"O how love I thy law! it is my meditation all the day. Thou through thy commandments hast made me wiser than mine enemies: for they are ever with me. I have more understanding than all my teachers: for thy testimonies are my meditations. I understand more than the ancients, because I keep thy precepts. I have refrained my feet from every evil way, that I might keep thy word. I have not departed from thy judgments: for thou hast taught me. How sweet are thy words unto my taste! yea, sweeter than honey to my mouth! Through thy precepts I get understanding: therefore I hate every false way."

King David knew the source of his strength and how to tap into that redemptive power. Let the words of my mouth, and the meditation of my heart, be acceptable in thy sight, O Lord, my strength, and my redeemer" (Psalm 19:14).

He knew he was not perfect and the only way to perfection was through the law of the Lord. "The law of the Lord is perfect, converting the soul: the testimony of the Lord is sure, making wise the simple" (Psalm 19:7).

When the king declared in Psalm 27:1, "The Lord is my light and my salvation; whom shall I fear? The Lord is the strength of my life; of whom shall I be afraid?" he was not talking about beholding the Lord face-to-face physically or spiritually speaking. He was talking about the law of the Lord that is both light and salvation to the soul of man. This kind of wisdom only comes from knowing and understanding his will.

The good news is that King David is not exclusive. We all can become people after God's heart. We also have the same rights and access as King David did, and even more so because of the work that Jesus Christ did for us at the cross of Calvary and because of the gift of the Holy Spirit. Christians can recognize the oracle of the Word of GOD; in Psalm 19:7. "The law of the LORD is perfect, converting the soul: the testimony of the LORD is sure, making wise the simple." And if we can desire to seek out all the glory of God (by reading, studying, and meditating on the Word of God). The Lord will lavish upon us power and glory to do exploits for Him in this our dispensation. If born-again Christians will turn to the Word of God to know His will, understand His ways, obtain wisdom, live in the fear of the Lord, and walk in obedience, everyone will experience a revival and turn the world upside down for our God.

The Word of God has been an oracle throughout history. It is the truth revealed through God, whether by means of the written word or the incarnate Word (our Savior and Messiah). Christ Jesus is the truth.

In creation, God made all things for His pleasure. "Thou art worthy, O LORD, to receive glory honor and power: for thou hast created all things, and for thy pleasure, they are and were created" (Revelation 4:11). Everything was made by Him. "For by Him were all things created, that are in heaven, that are in earth, visible and invisible, whether they be thrones, or dominions, or principalities, or powers: all things were created by Him, and for Him: And He is before all things, and by Him all things consist. And He is the head of the body, the church: who is the beginning, the first born from the dead; that in all things He might have the preeminence" (Colossians 1:16–18).

As stated in Genesis 1:1-3, "In the beginning GOD created the heaven and the earth. And the earth was without form, and void; and darkness was upon the face of the deep. And the Spirit of GOD moved upon the face of the waters. And GOD said, let there be light: and there was light."

He created all things by the power of His Word. "Hath in these last days spoken unto us by His son, whom He hath anointed heir of all things, by whom also He made the world; Who being the brightness of His glory, and the express image of His person, and upholding all things by the word of His power, when He had by Himself purged our sins, sat on the right hand of the majesty on high" (Hebrew 1:2–3). And He created man to serve Him, even though we cannot see, yet through His revealed glory and power, we will believe in Him and do His will. We are to draw out our hearts to seek His purpose. The secret is that this is to be a living experience each day. We have His Word to help us achieve this. "Sanctify them through thy truth: thy word is truth" (John 17:17). The Creator came to show the way. "Jesus saith unto him, I am the way, the truth, and the life: no one cometh unto the Father, but by me" (John 14:6). Jesus came to show the way back to the Father. He is the incarnate Word of God, the truth, and all life consists in Him. He has set the standard for us all. He has died in our place, and when we believe in Him and live the life that He has shown unto us, the life of God flows into our lives, and we operate in His power. He is coming back again to take those who have overcome, home from this world and all the deception in it to His heavenly kingdom.

> And I saw a new heaven and a new earth: for the first heaven and the first earth were passed away; and there was no more sea. And I John saw the holy city, new Jerusalem, coming down from God out of heaven, prepared as a bride adorned for her husband. And I heard a great voice out of heaven saying, Behold, the tabernacle of God is with men, and he will dwell with them, and they shall be his people, and God himself shall be with them, and be their God. And God shall wipe away all tears from their eyes; and there shall be no more death, neither sorrow, nor crying, neither shall there be any more pain: for the former things are passed away. And he that sat upon the throne said, Behold, I make all things new.

And he said unto me, Write: for these words are true and faithful. (Revelation 21:1–5)

Now consider Revelation 22:1–5:

> And he shewed me a pure river of water of life, clear as crystal, proceeding out of the throne of God and of the Lamb. In the midst of the street of it, and on either side of the river, was there the tree of life, which bare twelve manner of fruits, and yielded her fruit every month: and the leaves of the tree were for the healing of the nations. And there shall be no more curse: but the throne of God and of the Lamb shall be in it; and his servants shall serve him: And they shall see his face; and his name shall be in their foreheads. And there shall be no night there; and they need no candle, neither light of the sun; for the Lord God giveth them light: and they shall reign for ever and ever.

Throughout the Holy Bible, we see the Lord Himself had ordered the events that made history throughout the existence of man since creation. In hindsight, we see how man fell and how the curse of death came into the world. How wickedness and pride took over man and what man did was continually evil, as we can read from the following scripture. "And GOD saw that the wickedness of man was great in the earth, and that every imagination of the thoughts of his heart was only evil continually" (Genesis 6:5). And the Lord could not stand man and decided to destroy all mankind, but He spared a family of eight, Noah, his wife, his three sons, and their wives. "And it repented the LORD that He had made man on the earth, and it grieved Him at His heart. And the LORD said, I will destroy man whom I have created from the face of the earth; both man and beast, and the creeping thing, and the fowls of the air; for it repented me that I have made them. But Noah found grace in the eyes of the LORD" (Genesis 6:6–8).

How He ordered the confusion of the language of man, in other to frustrate the building of the tower of Babel, that was intended to reach heavens, and scattered man thoughout the earth "Go to, let us go down, and there confound their language, that they may not understand one another's speech. So the LORD scattered them abroad form thence upon the face of all the earth: and they left off to build the city. Therefore is the name of it called Babel: because the LORD did there confound the language of all the earth: and then from thence did the LORD scatter them abroad upon the face of all the earth" (Genesis 11:7–9).

And then He intended to raise a nation unto Himself and hence the call of Abraham. "Now the LORD had said unto Abram. Get thee out of thy country, and from thy kindred, and from thy father's house, unto a land I will show thee: And I will make of thee a great nation, and I will bless thee, and make thy name great; and thou shalt be a blessing: And I will bless them that bless thee, and curse him that curseth thee: and in thee shall all the families of the earth be blessed" (Genesis 12:1–3).

God pronounced His blessing on Abraham.

> And the LORD said unto Abram, after that Lot was separated from him, lift up now thine eyes, and look from the place where thou art northward, and southward, and eastward, and westward: For all the land which thou seest, to thee will I give, and to thy seed forever. And I will make thy seed as the dust of the earth: so that if a man can number the dust of the earth, then shall thy seed also be numbered. Arise, walk through the land in the length of it and in the breadth of it; for I will give it unto thee. Then Abram removed his tent, and came and dwelt in the plain of Mamre, which is in Hebron, and built there an alter unto the LORD. (Genesis 13:14–18)

Consider next Genesis 15:18–21. "In the same day the LORD made a covenant with Abram, saying, Unto thy seed have I given this land, from the river of Egypt unto the great river, the river Euphrates: The Kenites, and the Kenizzites, and the Kadmonites, and the Hittites, and the Perizites, and the Rephaims, and the Amorites, and the Canaanites, and the Girgashites, and the Jebusites."

And then read Genesis 15:1–6, which says,

> After these things the word of the LORD came unto Abram in a vision, saying, fear not, Abram: I am thy shield, and thy exceeding great reward. And Abram said, LORD GOD, what wilt thou give me, seeing I go childless, and the steward of my house is this Eliezer of Damascus? And Abram said, Behold, to me thou hast given no seed: and, lo, one born in my house is mine heir. And, behold, the word of the LORD came unto him, saying, This shall not be thine heir; but he that shall come forth out of thine own bowels shall be thine heir. And he brought him forth abroad, and said, look now towards heaven, and tell the stars, if thou be able to number them: and he said unto him, so shall thy seed be. And he believed in the LORD; and he counted it to him for righteousness.

The Lord told Abraham of Israel's bondage in a dream.

> And he said unto him, I am the LORD that brought thee out of Ur of the Chaldees, to give thee this land to inherit it. And he said, LORD GOD, whereby shall I know that I shall inherit it. And he said unto him, take me a heifer of three years old, and she goat of three years old, and a ram of three years old, and a turtledove, and a pigeon. And he took unto him all these, and divided them in the midst, and laid each piece one against another: but the birds divided he not. And when the fowls came down

upon the carcasses, Abram drove them away. And when the sun was going down, a deep sleep fell upon Abram; and , lo, a horror of great darkness fell upon him. And He said unto Abram, know of a surety that thy seed shall be a stranger in a land that is not theirs, and shall serve them; and they shall afflict them four hundred years; and also that nation, whom they shall serve, will I judge: and afterward shall they come out with great substance. And thou shalt go to thy fathers in peace; thou shalt be buried in a good old age. But in the fourth generation they shall come hither again: for the iniquity of the Amorites is not yet full. And it came to pass, that, when the sun went down, and it was dark, behold a smoking furnace, and a burning lamp that passed between those pieces. (Genesis. 15:7–17)

The Lord also promised Sarah a child at the age of eighty-nine.

And they said unto him, where is Sarah thy wife? And he said, behold in the tent. And He said, I will certainly return unto thee according to the time of life; and, lo, Sarah thy wife shall have a son. And Sarah heard it in the tent door, which was behind him. Now Abraham and Sarah were old and well stricken in age; and it ceased to be with Sarah after the manner of women. Therefore Sarah laughed within herself, saying, After I am waxed old shall I have pleasure, my lord being old also? And the LORD said unto Abraham, wherefore did Sarah laugh, saying, shall I of a surety bear a child, which am old? Is anything too hard for the LORD? At the time appointed I will return unto thee, according to the time of life, and Sarah shall have a son. Then Sarah denied, saying, I laughed not: for she was afraid, And he said, Nay; but thou didst laugh. (Genesis 18:9–15)

Then the birth of Isaac transpired.

> And the LORD visited Sarah as He had said, and
> the LORD did unto Sarah as He had spoken. For Sarah
> conceived, and bare Abraham a son in his old age, at the
> set time of which GOD had spoken to him. And Abraham
> called the name of his son that was born unto him, whom
> Sarah bare to him, Isaac. And Abraham circumcised his
> son Isaac being eight days old, as GOD had commanded
> him. And Abraham was a hundred years old, when his
> son Isaac was born to unto him. And Sarah said, GOD
> hath made me to laugh, so all that hear will laugh with
> me. And she said, who would have said unto Abraham,
> that Sarah should have been given children suck? For I
> have born him a son in his old age. And the child grew,
> and was weaned: and Abraham made a great feast the
> same day that Isaac was weaned. (Genesis 21:1–8)

The wicked Sodom and Gomorrah was then destroyed in Genesis
18:16–21.

> "And the men rose up from thence, and look toward
> Sodom: and Abraham went with them to bring them on
> the way. And the LORD said, shall I hide from Abraham
> that thing which I do; Seeing that Abraham shall surely
> become a great and mighty nation, and all nations of
> the earth shall be blessed in him. For I know him, that
> he will command his children and his household after
> him, and they shall keep the way of the LORD, to do
> justice and judgment; that the LORD may bring upon
> Abraham that which he hath spoken of him. And the
> LORD said, Because the cry of Sodom and Gomorrah
> is great, and because their sin is very grievous; I will go
> down now, and see whether they have done altogether

according to the cry of it, which is come unto me; and
if not, I will know."

We all know how the story of Sodom and Gomorrah ended (you
can look that up in Genesis 19: 24 -29). The Lord because he has
not changed will see to it that every word he has ever uttered is
fulfilled, whether to individuals or to a nation or to the world as a
whole. Like the separation of a nation for Himself, and the others
to the contrary; God has promised His people an eternal reign with
Him in His Kingdom, but an everlasting condemnation in a lake of
unquenchable fire to the rest.

> "He also that had received two talents, came and said,
> LORD, thou deliveredst unto me two talents: behold, I
> have gained two other talents beside them. His lord said
> unto him, well done, good and faithful servant; thou has
> been faithful over a few things, I will make thee ruler over
> many things; enter thou into the joy of thy lord" (Matthew
> 25:22–23).

A day of reckoning is coming when all shall give account of their
stewardship, those that do well shall be called "good and faithful
servant" and welcome to enter into the joy of the Lord. But those
that will not do well, shall be cast into eternal condemnation. Which
one will you be? Hear what the word of the Lord says about the
separation of two people in the book of Malachi:

"The burden of the word of the LORD to Israel by Malachi. "I
have loved you, saith the LORD. Yet ye say, wherein hast thou loved
us? Was not Esau Jacob's brother? saith the LORD: yet I loved Jacob,
3. And I hated Esau, and laid his mountains and his heritage waste
for the dragons of the wilderness" (Malachi 1:1–3).

The Lord has set us apart for Himself because He loves us, there
will also be a fulfillment of the separation of those that reject the
love of God and hence were rejected by God.

"As it is written, Jacob have I loved, but Esau have I hated" (Romans 9:13).

"GOD is not a man, that He should lie; neither the son of man that He should repent: hath He said, and shall He not do it? Or hath he spoken, and shall he not make it good?" (Numbers 23:19).

From this scripture, it is evident that whatever the Lord says, He also does. Whatever He has spoken about, He makes good also. In other words, whatever the Lord declares bears His creative power to bring that thing, situation, or circumstance to pass. Just as in creation, everything that the Lord God declared stands. And throughout history, His word has never failed.

The good news about the Word of GOD is that it can never become obsolete. It is ever-relevant. "For the word of GOD is quick, and powerful, and shaper that any two- edged sword, piercing even to the dividing asunder of soul and spirit, and of joints and marrow, and is a discerner of the thoughts and intents of the heart" (Hebrews 4:12). When we live lives that are pleasing to God and we appropriate His Word, it comes to pass. No matter what the situation is, it might look impossible from the human perspective. When a faithful child of God recognizes what the Lord says concerning any situation or circumstance and appropriates it, there is a result, and the Word of God stands.

The Lord God is a covenant-keeping God. He is much more interested in making good everything that He has spoken about than He is concerned about setting new standards. As it is written in Psalm 105:8–15,

> He hath remembered His covenant forever, the word which He commanded to a thousand generations. Which covenant He made with Abraham, and His oath unto Isaac; And confirm the same unto Jacob for a law, and to Israel for an everlasting covenant. Saying, unto thee will I give the land of Canaan, the lot of your inheritance: When they were but a few men in number; yea, very few,

and strangers in it. When they went from one nation to another, from one kingdom to another people; He suffered no man to do them wrong: yea, He reproved kings for their sakes; Saying touch not my anointed and do my prophet no harm.

This is why, when He says, "Return unto me, and I will return unto you." He means His Word, which is His oath to us. "For I am the LORD, I change not; therefore ye sons of Jacob are not consumed. Even from the days of your fathers ye have gone away from mine ordinances, and have not kept them. Return unto me, and I will return unto you, saith the LORD of Hosts. But ye said, wherein shall we return" (Malachi 3:6–7). His oath of death to the sinners or eternal life to the righteous shall all come to pass.

As I live, saith the LORD GOD, ye shall not have occasion any more to use this proverb in Israel. Behold, all souls are mine; as the soul of the father, so also the soul of the son is mine; the soul that sinneth, it shall die. But if a man be just, and do that which is lawful and right. And hath not eaten upon the mountains, neither hath lifted up his eyes to the idols of the house of Israel, neither hath defiled his neighbor's wife, neither hath come near a menstruous woman. And hath not oppressed any, but hath restored to the debtor his pledge, hath spoiled none by violence, hath given his bread to the hungry, and hath covered the naked with a garment; He that hath not given forth upon usury, neither hath taken any increase, that hath withdrawn his hand from iniquity, hath executed true judgment between man and man, hath walked in my statutes, and hath kept my judgment, to deal truly; he is just, he shall surely live, saith the LORD GOD. (Ezekiel 18:3–9)

The Bible is clear about the eternal relevance of the Word of God. "This book of the law shall not depart out of thy mouth; but thou shall meditate therein day and night, that thou mayest observe to do according to all that is written therein: for then thou shalt make thy way prosperous, and then thou shall have good success" (Joshua 1:8).

One should also consider the following two passages: "So shall my word be that goeth forth out of my mouth: it shall not return unto me void, but it shall accomplish that which I please, and it shall prosper in the thing whereto I send it" (Isaiah 55:11). "And this is the record, that GOD hath given to us eternal life, and this life is in His son" (1 John 5:13).

The Holy Scripture is the infallible, inerrant Word of God that is ever-relevant. "But continue thou in the things which thou hast learned and hast been assured of, knowing of whom thou hast learned them. And that from a child thou hast known the Holy scriptures, which are able to make thee wise unto salvation through faith which is in Christ Jesus. All scripture is given by inspiration of GOD, and is profitable for doctrine, for reproof, for correction, for instruction in righteousness: That the man of GOD may be perfect, thoroughly furnished unto all good works" (2 Timothy 3:14–17).

There is life and power in God's Word. Hence, its relevance to all generation. If we are serious about revival in this our dispensation, we must read and study the Word of God daily and meditate on it each day and night. The power of God in His Word will come to pass in our situations, circumstances, and needs.

Every prophecy in the Holy Scripture has been fulfilled, except for the second coming of our Lord and Savior, Jesus Christ, and the events that will follow. Therefore, we can trust that everything that the Lord declared through His prophets will come to pass in our own lives.

> The Spirit of the Lord God is upon me , because the
> Lord hath anointed me to preach the good tidings unto
> the meek, he hath sent me to bind up the broken-hearted,

to proclaim liberty to the captives, and the opening of the prison to them that are bound. To proclaim the acceptable year of the Lord, and the day of vengeance of our God; to comfort them that mourn". (Isaiah 61:1–3).

This prophecy is fulfilled in Christ Jesus in Luke 4:18-19. "The Spirit of the Lord is upon me, because he has anointed me to preach the gospel to the poor; he hath sent me to heal the broken-hearted." To preach deliverance to the captives, and the recovering of sight to the blind. To set at liberty them those are bruised. To preach the acceptable year of the Lord."

Every scripture has been fulfilled a million times over and can be fulfilled in your life as well, if only you will sacrifice the time to read, study, and meditate on the Word of God, and just believe it.

It is recommended that we read at least three chapters of the Bible every day of our lives, and we should read through the Bible at least once every year for the rest of our lives. But when we are reading, if we can also study God's Word daily, take up topics like forgiveness and its importance, and vow to live in obedience, we will begin to see the Word of God working out His purpose in our lives. Through the answers, messages and burdens that comes from knowing His word (will).

As it says in Joel 2:28, "And it shall come to pass afterward, that I will pour out my spirit upon all flesh; and your sons your daughters shall prophecy, and your old men shall dream dreams, your young men shall see vision." The promise of the Lord through the prophet Joel was fulfilled on the day of Pentecost, when the disciples were baptized with the Holy Ghost and fire. You can count on every word of the prophecy, knowing that the Lord God always does whatever He says and He always make good on everything He has spoken.

The oracle of God's Word is the answer to everything about life and Godliness.

"Simon Peter, a servant and an apostle of JESUS CHRIST, to them that have obtained like precious faith with us through the righteousness of GOD and our savior JESUS CHRIST: Grace and peace be multiplied unto you through the knowledge of GOD, and of JESUS our LORD. According to His divine power hath given unto us all things that pertain unto life and godliness, through the knowledge of Him that hath called us to glory and virtue: Whereby are given unto us exceeding great and precious promises: that by these ye might be partakers of the divine nature, having escaped the corruption that is in the world through lust." (2 Peter 1:1–4)

Through the knowledge of our God that the Holy Scripture stands for, we have access to His divine power, that has given us all things that pertain to life and godliness, to live above the corruption That is in the world. Through the knowledge of Him, we are given exceeding great and precious promises. Thereby, we become partakers of the His divine nature. The oracle of God's Word is the answer for all that is good and evil, blessing and cursing, life and death.

In that I command thee this day to love the LORD thy GOD, to walk in His ways, and to keep His commandments, that thou mayest live and multiply: and the LORD thy GOD shall bless thee in the land whither thou goest to possess it. But if thine heart turn away, so that thou wilt not hear, but shalt be drawn away, and worship other gods, and serve them; I denounce unto you this day, that ye shall surely perish, and that you shall not prolong your days upon the land, wither thou passest over Jordan to go to possess it. I call heaven and earth to record this day against you, that I have set before you life and death, blessings and cursing: therefore choose life, that both thou and thy seed may live: That thou mayest love the LORD thy GOD, and that thou mayest obey His voice, and that thou mayest cleave unto Him:

for He is thy life, and the length of thy days: that thou mayest dwell in the land which the LORD sware unto thy fathers, to Abraham, to Isaac, and to Jacob, to give them. (Deuteronomy 30:16–20)

When we do what the Lord wants, when we walk in His ways proactively and keep His commandments and His statutes, we are bound to experience the abundant life that Jesus promised us. The Lord Himself will bless us wherever we are and wherever we may go. But when we do the contrary or even when we are just passive, we have chosen evil and death ultimately. The oracle of God's Word is a reliable and sure guide for a prosperous and a successful life. "This book of the law shall not depart out of thy mouth; but thou shall meditate therein day and night, that thou mayest observe to do according to all that is written therein: for then thou shalt make thy way prosperous, and then thou shall have good success" (Joshua 1:8).

Are you a born-again Christian and want more in the kingdom of God (the church) or even in your life? You have an oracle (the Holy Bible) in your hand. Start consulting. Start searching the Scriptures day and night with a heart set on obeying His Word. Apply it in your day-to-day living. This is what is recorded about his situation at one point in David's life: "Then David and the people that were with him lifted up their voice and wept, until they had no more power to weep. And David's two wives were taken captives, Ahinoam the Jezreelites, and Abigail the wife of Nabal the Carmelite. And David was greatly distressed; for the people spake of stoning him, because the soul of all the people was grieved, every man for his sons and for his daughters" (1 Samuel 30:4–6). But David encouraged himself in the Lord, his God. I recommend that you read the whole story in 1 Samuel 30 and see for yourself how David was able to overcome such disaster. The Lord might as well be telling you right now to pursue your enemies, for thou shall surely overtake and recover all.

Chapter 3

THE ORACLE OF PRAYER

Ask and it shall be given you; seek, and ye shall find; knock and it shall be open unto you: For everyone that asketh receiveth; and he that seeketh findeth; and to him that knocketh it shall be opened. Or what man is there of you, whom if his son ask bread, will he give him a stone? Or if he ask a fish, will he give him a serpent? If ye then, being evil, know how to give good gifts unto your children, how much more shall your heavenly Father which is in heaven give good things to them that ask Him.
—Matthew 7:7–11

Prayer is the only active exercise in life that engages the Lord God in the moment. "And it shall come to pass, that before they call, I will answer; and while they are yet speaking, I will hear" (Isaiah 65:24). Prayer gives you unrestrained access to His infinitesimal power and gives His power access to everything that concerns you. In prayer, you can alter the events of the universe or your life. In Joshua 10:12–14, the Bible says,

> Then spake Joshua to the LORD in the day when the LORD delivered up the Amorites before the children of Israel, and he said in the sight of the Israel, sun, stand thou still upon Gibeon; and thou, moon, in the valley of

Ajalon. And the sun stood still, and the moon stayed, until the people had avenged themselves upon their enemies. Is not this written in the book of Jasher? So the sun stood still in the midst of heaven, and hasted not to go down about a whole day. And there was no day like that before it or after it, that the LORD hearkened unto the voice of a man: for the LORD fought for Israel.

As it says in Jeremiah 33:3, "Call unto me, and I will answer thee, and show thee great and mighty things, which thou knowest not."

When we pray, we go before God to plead our cases in that moment. He has promised us unconditional access. He goes to work in response to what we place before Him. God has given us this access so that we can engage Him at any time of the day anywhere, and there is no other way around it. Wishes will not work. When we deny ourselves prayer, we rob ourselves of the opportunity to engage the Almighty God in our struggles, needs, or battles, and our enemy is the one that wins. This is why the Enemy will do anything to make sure that we do not pray. So many doubt their ability to pray. Others feel they are not good enough, and still others have a lack of understanding. If only we could understand the grace of God in prayer and the power available to us, we would pray without ceasing. We would engage the Lord at all times and in all situations, small or big, spiritual or physical, and things would change for our good and for His praise.

God wants you to engage Him in the issues of your life anytime, every time; that access is open for you, even now. "And call upon me in the day of trouble: I will deliver thee, and thou shalt glorify me" (Psalm 50:15).

Prayerlessness is like leaving a deep open wound untreated and wishing and hoping that it will go away. We live in a world where bad things only tend to become worse unless you do something about them. Prayerlessness will leave you at the mercy of the elements, which only corrodes and makes things worse. You will be left to the mercy of miserable comforters. Who will only highlight your failures and your unpardonable mistakes and sins. But God will not do that to you when you engage Him through prayer as He said in 2 Chronicles 7:14. "If my people, which are called by my name, shall humble themselves, and pray, and seek my face, and turn from their wicked ways; then I will hear from heaven, and will forgive their sins, and will heal their land." And it is also written in verses 15 and 16 that "His eyes are open, His ears attent, His heart and arms are open for you to run into His embrace and comfort. "Now my eyes shall be open, and mine ears attent unto the prayer that is made in this place. For now have I chosen and sanctified this house, that my name may be there forever: and mine eyes and mine heart shall be there perpetually." (2 Chronicles 7: 15-16)

Prayer is the only door that you can personally open in order to engage the Almighty Father, and He will always be there every hour of every day. Consider Hannah in Samuel 1:1–18:

> Now there was a certain man of Remathaim, of mount Ephraim, and his name was Elkanah, the son of Jeroham, the son of Elihu, the son of Tohu, the son of Zuph, an Ephrathite: And he had two wives; the name of the one was Hannah, and the name of the other Peninnah: and Peninnah had children, but Hannah had no children. And this man went up out of his city yearly to worship and to sacrifice unto the LORD of Hosts in Shiloh. And the two sons of Eli, Hophni and Phinehas, the priest of the LORD, were there. And when the time was that Elkanah offered, he gave to Peninah his wife, and to al her sons and her daughters, portions: But unto Hannah he gave a worthy portion; for he loved Hannah: but the LORD had shut up her womb. And her adversary also provoked her sore, for to make her fret, because the LORD had shut up her womb. And as he did so year by year, when she went up to the house of the LORD, so she provoked her;

therefore she wept, and did not eat. Then said Elkanah her husband to her, "Hannah, why weepest thu? And why eatest thou not? And why is thy heart grieved? Am not I better to thee than ten sons?" So Hannah rose up after they had eaten in Shiloh, and after they had drunk. Now Eli the priest sat upon a seat by a post of the temple of the LORD. And she was in bitterness of soul, and prayed unto the LORD, and wept sore. And she vowed a vow, and said, O LORD of Hosts, if thou wilt indeed look on the affliction of thine handmaid, and remember me, and not forget thine handmaid, but wilt give unto thine handmaid a man child, then I will give him unto the LORD all the days of his life, and there shall no razor come upon his head. And it came to pass, as she continue praying before the LORD, that Eli marked her mouth. Now Hannah, she spake in her heart; only her lips moved, but her voice was not heard: therefore Eli thought she had been drunken, and Eli said unto her, hoe long wilt thou be drunken? Put away thy wine from thee. And Hannah answered and said, No, my LORD, I am a woman of a sorrowful spirit: I have drunk neither wine nor strong drink, but have poured out my soul before the LORD. Count not thine handmaid for a daughter of Belial: for out of the abundance of my complaint and grief have I spoken hitherto. The Eli answered and said, Go in peace: and the GOD of Israel grant thy petition that thou hast asked of Him. And she said, Let thine handmaid find grace in thy sight. So the woman went her way, and did eat, and her countenance was no more sad.

Without help from anyone else, Hannah personally opened that door and walked through that door to engage the Lord. When her mate was raining insults on her, when her husband's consolation was not helpful, when the high priest, the only mediator of the time between God and man, could not help her, she engaged God one-on-one, and the rest was history. Beloved, you will not understand how much you have lost and stand to lose by just reading this or any other book or by hearing any message on prayer until prayer becomes part of you. At this time, I strongly suggest you pray these three prayer points. Pray each prayer point for ten minutes.

1. Oh, Lord, my Father, arise and break down and totally destroy every prayer barrier and oppositions in my life in the name of Jesus.

2. Oh, Lord, my God, awaken in me, my prayer eagle, in Jesus' mighty name.

3. Father Lord, give me a reason to pray all the days of my life in the mighty name of Jesus.

There is a saying in my native land that goes like this: "When you enter where they produce red oil (palm oil), you will surely be stained by red oil." In other words, when you enter into where they produce this red oil, it will touch you somehow, or you might bump into something with the oil, because everything in that house has a palm oil stain. Because you are in His presence and because he filleth all in all. When you pray personally in Jesus' name, no minister, no angels, just you and the Father, you will be touched by Him in one way or another. "And whatsoever ye shall ask in my name, that will I do, that the Father may be glorified in the Son. If ye shall ask anything in my name, I will do it" (John 14:13–14).

Jesus is the mediator between us and the Father. Thus, every prayer must be offered in the name of Jesus. He is our High Priest, who has offered up the only acceptable sacrifice. "And all things, whatsoever ye shall ask in prayer, believing, ye shall receive" (Matthew 21:22).

Here, see how much importance the Lord attaches to prayer. "All things, whatsoever" means is all-inclusive. Therefore, in order to receive things that are naturally out of your reach, things that man will physically deny you, or things that invisible forces have made impossible for you to reach, prayer is the only activity that can make impossibilities possible, because it engages God. Weeping, self-pity, and sympathy seeking will only open you up and make you more vulnerable to the forces of abuse.

There are things that you cannot buy your way into or buy your way out of, no matter how much money you have, it does not matter if you are the richest man on earth. But in the words of Jesus in Matthew 21:22, "And all things, whatsoever ye shall ask in prayer, believing, ye shall receive." This is serious business, so if you are a child of God rich in His Word, you can prove this to be true just by engaging in prayer for all things, and you will see the power of God in your life and working through your life.

Prayer is the singular activity available to mankind to directly engage the Almighty and access His power to work for us and through us, and when prayer is done according to the purpose of God, we will get the answers that we desire and can also surpass our desires; however, we will come short otherwise. "Ye lust, and have not: ye kill, and desire to have, and cannot obtain: ye fight and war, yet ye have not, because ye ask not. 3. Ye ask, and receive not, because ye ask amiss, that ye may consume it upon your lusts" (James 4:2–3). Either way we short-change ourselves, when we fail to pray or when we pray the wrong prayers. Prayer is a must but also must be said only in God's accepted standards, the Lord will only answer a prayer when it is according to his will and when it comes from an obedient child of God. We cannot force God's hand to do anything against His will, whatever you pray for must be in accordance with His will. Our Lord and savior prayed often and all His prayers were in agreement with the will of His heavenly father. He never prayed amiss and was very obedient to His father. The Bible is pretty clear of how often Jesus prayed hence the standard He has set for us all.

The Examples of Jesus in Prayer

While He was here on earth, Jesus was always praying. He always participated in the singular activity available to man that allowed people to engage God the Father and the authority of His kingdom. While He was here in the flesh, it was not enough that He was the only begotten Son of God. Because He was here, He has to use the only channel available to man. Jesus was always praying. Consider the following passages:

> And in the morning, rising up a great while before day, he went out, and departed into a solitary place, and there prayed. (Mark 1:35)

> And when He had sent them away, he departed into a mountain to pray. (Mark 6:46)

> And He withdrew Himself into the wilderness, and prayed. (Luke 5:16)

> And it came to pass in those days, that He went out into a mountain to pray, and continue all night in prayer to GOD. (Luke 6:12)

> And it came to pass about eight days after these sayings He took Peter and John and James, and went up into a mountain to pray. And as He prayed, the fashion of His countenance was altered, and His raiment was white and glistering. (Luke 9:28–29)

> And it came to pass, that, as He was praying in a certain place, when He ceased, one of His disciples said unto Him, LORD, teach us to pray, as John also taught His disciples. (Luke 11:1)

> Who in the days of His flesh, when He had offered up prayers and supplications with strong crying and tears

49

unto Him that was able to save Him in that he feared. Though He were a Son, yet learned He obedience by the things which He suffered. (Hebrew 5:7–8)

Jesus was always praying. This is why He was so full of power to heal the sick, cast out demons, and work miracles without number. Jesus was the greatest prayer warrior that lived, and if the only begotten Son of God prayed as He did, you and I have no excuse and failure to pray and master the art of praying, is gross negligence and can be very costly. I believe that we all need to become prayer warriors like our Savior and Master.

Jesus understood the oracle of prayer while He was here in the flesh, and that is why He taught His disciples how to pray in so many different ways. For example, when a certain man brought his lunatic child (son) to Jesus' disciples and they could not minister deliverance to the child, they asked Jesus why they had failed. Here is what ensued:

> And when they were come to the multitude, there came to Him a certain man, kneeling down to Him, and saying, LORD, have mercy on my son; for he is lunatic, and sore vexed: for oftentimes he falleth into the fire, and oft into the water. And I brought him to thy disciples, and they could not cure him, then JESUS answered and said, O faithless and perverse generation, how long shall I be with you? How long shall I suffer you? Bring him hither to me, and JESUS rebuke the devil; and he departed out of him: and the child was cured from that very hour. Then came the disciples to JESUS apart, and said, why could not we cast him out? And JESUS said unto them, Because of your unbelief: for verily I say unto you, if you have faith as a grain of mustard seed, ye shall say unto this mountain, remove hence to yonder place; and it shall be remove; and nothing shall be impossible unto you.

Howbeit this kind goeth not out but by prayer and fasting. (Matthew 17:14–21)

In Mark 11:12–26, the Bible says the following:

And on the morrow, when they were come to Bethany, He was hungry: And seeing a fig tree afar off having leaves, He came, if haply he might find anything thereon: and when He came to it, He found nothing but leaves: for the time of figs was not yet. And JESUS answered and said unto it. No man eats fruit of thee hereafter forever. And His disciples heard it. And they came to Jerusalem: and JESUS went into the temple, and began to cast out them that sold and bought in the temples, and over threw the table of the money changers, and the seat of them that sold doves; And would not suffer that any man should carry any vessel through the temple. And He taught, saying unto them, Is it not written, my house shall be called of all nations the house of prayer? But ye have made it a den of thieves. And the scribes and the chief priests heard it, and sought how they might destroy Him: for they feared Him, because all the people were astonished at His doctrine. And when even was come, He went out of the city. And in the morning, as they passed by, they saw the fig tree dried up from the roots. And Peter calling to remembrance saith unto Him, Master, behold, the fig tree which thou cursedst is withered away. And JESUS answering saith unto them, have faith in GOD. For verily I say unto you. That whosoever shall say unto this mountain, Be thou removed, and be thou cast into the sea; and shall not doubt in his heart, but shall believe that those things which he saith shall come to pass; he shall have whatsoever he saith. Therefore I say unto you, what things soever ye desire, when ye pray,

believe that ye receive them, and ye shall have them. And
when ye stand praying, forgive, if you had aught against
any: that your Father also which is in heaven may forgive
you your trespasses. But if ye do not forgive, neither will
your Father which in heaven forgive your trespasses.

Here, the Lord used the incident of the fig tree cursing to
emphasize the oracle of prayer, particularly in verse 24. This is what
the Lord taught us in this parable about a judge in a certain city.

And He spake a parable unto them to this end, that
men ought always to pray, and not to faint: Saying, there
was in a city a judge, which feared not GOD, neither
regarded man: And there was a widow in that city; and
she came unto him, saying, Avenge me of mine adversary.
And he would not for a while: but afterward he said
within himself, Though I fear not GOD, nor regard man;
Yet because this widow troubleth me, I will avenge her,
lest by her continual coming she weary me. And the
LORD said, Hear what the unjust judge saith, and shall
not GOD avenge His own elect, which cry day and night
unto Him, though He bear long with them? I tell you
that He will avenge them speedily. Nevertheless when
the son of man cometh, shall He find faith on the earth?
(Luke 18:1–8)

Prayer is supposed to be done each day and night. Nevertheless,
shall I find anyone faithful in the area of prayer? Here, Jesus is
showing us that prayer, when it is done persistently, can change the
hardest of situations. But we need to direct the question in verse 8
to ourselves. Will the Lord find us faithful if He returns today?

Is your pastor, bishop, or priest very prayerful? That is good. Is your
church a prayerful church that is excellent? But the most important
question you can ask yourself today is this: Are you prayerful? The

Lord expects you to pray. If the individual Christian prays each day and night, the church of God will be untouchable, and when we come together, heaven will come down. Do you desire the touch of God in your life and circumstances? Do you desire an awakening in your life or a revival in your life? Do you desire revival in your church or the body of Christ in general? Do not wait any longer for an anointed hand to be laid upon you or for a revival to break forth somewhere so that you can go and join them and become a partaker. Instead, engage God through the means of prayer, His powerful oracle. James put it this way in James 5:13–18:

> Is any among you afflicted? Let him pray. Is any merry? Let him sing psalms. Is any sick among you? Let him call for the elders of the church; and let them pray over him, anointing him with oil in the name of the LORD. And the prayer of faith shall save the sick, and the LORD shall raise him up; and if he have committed sins, they shall be forgiven him. Confess your fault one to another, and pray for one another, that ye may be healed. The effectual fervent prayer of the righteous man availeth much. Elias was a man subject to like passions as we are, and he prayed earnestly that it might not rain: and it rained not on the earth by the space of three years and six months. And he prayed again, and the heaven gave rain, and the earth brought forth her fruit.

The oracle of prayer is still active and will always be just as it was available to Elijah and Jabez and our Lord and Savior, Jesus Christ, in their days. So it is available to us today. All we need to do is become unsophisticated and humble ourselves and bend our knees in prayer, and revival will start like never before. Christians are looking for easy ways out. They have become too busy to pray. Preachers and ministers of God are looking for ways to make things easier for the congregations and their followers so that they will never have any need to pray. This is the problem of the church today. There is no easy way out. The Father did not make an easy way out for Jesus when He asked Him to "let this cup pass from me." Your desire and miracle are only a prayer away, but if you don't pray, do not expect anything to come through, because it will not happen. That is the sad truth. I remember several occasions when I have been cornered, when I was pushed to the wall and there was no minister to call or go to. During those times, I would fall on my knees and pray so fervently, and God would send an answer in the most powerful ways. When King Hezekiah received the most devastating message from his most trusted man of God, the Bible says he turned his face to the wall and prayed. Immediately, God changed the situation.

> In those days was Hezekiah sick unto death. And Isaiah the prophet the son of Amoz came unto him, and said unto him, Thus saith the LORD, Set thine house in order: for thou shalt die, and not live. Then Hezekiah turned his face toward the wall, and prayed unto the LORD. And said, Remember now, O LORD, I beseech thee, how I have walked before thee in truth and with a perfect heart, and have done that which is good in thy sight. And Hezekiah wept sore. Then came the word of the LORD to Isaiah, saying, Go, and say to Hezekiah, Thus saith the LORD, the GOD of David thy father, I have heard thy prayer, I have seen thy tears: behold, I will add unto thy days fifteen years. And I will deliver thee and this city out of the hand of the king of Assyria: and I will defend this city. And this shall be a sign unto thee from the LORD, that the LORD will do this thing that He hath spoken; Behold I will bring again the shadow of the degrees, which is gone down in the sun dial of Ahaz, ten degrees backward. So the sun returned ten degrees, by which degrees it was gone down. (Isaiah 38:1–8)

The oracle of prayer is the most powerful means available to man to unlock the doors of heaven and enter into the realm of the kingdom of God, where all things are possible.

There is no substitute for prayer!

Contrary to what some preachers will say in their church services, there is no substitute for prayer. Whether you need to break free from generational bondages, curses and covenant; or you need to receive healing from sickness, or you need God to provide during times of lack, there is no other way but through prayer. So many have died prematurely. Others have suffered heavy losses, and yet others have generational or foundational burdens all their lives that end up dragging them down. The only effective way to address any of these issues is through prayer. Consider Jabez in 1 Chronicles 4:9–10: "And Jabez was more honorable than his brethren: and his mother called his name Jabez, saying, Because I bare him in sorrow. And Jabez called on the GOD of Israel, saying, Oh that thou wouldest bless me indeed, and enlarge my coast, and that thine hand might be with me, and that thou wouldest keep me from evil, that it may not grieve me! And GOD granted him that which he requested."

God heard the prayer of Samson and granted him his heart's desire. Even after he disappointed God, he repented in Judges 16:23–31.

> Then the lords of the philistines gathered them together for to offer a great sacrifice unto dagon their god, and to rejoice: for they said, our god hath delivered Samson our enemy into our hand. And when the people saw him, they praised their god: for they said, our god hath delivered into our hands our enemy, and the destroyer of our country, which slew many of us. And it came to pass, when their hearts were merry, that they said, call for Samson, that he may make us sport. And they called

for Samson out of the prison house; and he made them sport: and they set him between the pillars. And Samson said unto the lad that held him by the hand; suffer me that I may feel the pillars whereupon the house standeth, that I may lean upon them. Now the house was full of men and women; and all the lords of the philistines were there; and they were upon the roof about three thousand men and women, that beheld while Samson made sport. And Samson called unto the LORD, and said, O LORD GOD, remember me, I pray thee, only this once, O GOD, that I may be at once avenged of the philistines for my two eyes. And Samson took hold of the two middle pillars upon which the house stood, and on which it was borne up, of the one with his right hand, and of the other with his left. And Samson said, let me die with the philistines. And he bowed himself with all his might; and the house fell upon the lords, and upon all the people that were therein. So the dead which he slew at his death were more than they he slew in his life. Then his brethren and all the house of his father came down, and buried him between Zorah and Eshtaol in the burial place of Manoah his father. And he Judged Israel for twenty years.

So too, the apostles prayed for the release of Peter from prison in Acts of the Apostles 12:1–19.

Now about that time Herod the king stretch forth his hands to vex certain of the church. And he killed James the brother of John with the sword. And because he saw it pleased the Jews, he proceeded further to take Peter also. (Then were the days of unleavened bread.) And when he had apprehended him, he put him in prison, and delivered him to four quaternion's of soldiers to keep him;

intending after Easter to bring him forth to the people. Peter therefore was kept in prison: but prayer was made without ceasing of the church unto GOD for him. And when Herod would have brought him forth, the same night Peter was sleeping between two soldiers, bound with two chains: and the keepers before the door kept the prison. And, behold, the angel of the LORD came upon him, and a light shined in the prison: and he smote Peter on the side, and raised him up, saying, Arise up quickly. And his chains fell off from his hands. And the angel said unto him, Gird thyself, and bind on thy sandals. And so he did. And he saith unto him, cast thy garment about thee, and follow me. And he went out, and followed him; and wist not that it was true which was done by the angel; but thought he saw a vision. When they were past the first and the second ward, they came unto the Iron gate that leadeth unto the city; which opened to them of his own accord: and they went out, and passed on through one street; and forth with the angel departed from him. And when Peter was come to himself, he said, Now I know of a surety, that the LORD hath sent his angel, and hath delivered me out of the hand of Herod, and all the expectation of the people of the Jews. And when he had considered the thing, he came to the house of Mary the mother of John, whose surname was Mark; where many were gathered together praying. And as Peter knocked at the door of the gate, a damsel came to hearken, named Rhoda. And when she knew Peter's voice, she opened not the gate for gladness, but ran in, and told how Peter stood before the gate. And they said unto her, Thou art mad. But she constantly affirmed that it was even so. Then said they, it is his angel. But Peter continued knocking; and when they had opened the door, and saw him, they were astonished. But he, motioning unto them with the hand to hold their peace, declared unto them how the LORD had brought him out of the prison. And he said, Go show these things unto James, and to the brethren. And he departed, and went into another place. Now as soon as it was day, there was no small stir among the soldiers, what was become of Peter. And when Herod had sought for him, and found him not, he examined the keepers, and commanded that they should be put to death. And he went down from Judea to Caesarea, and their abode.

Or how about when King Ahab prayed to the Lord to save Israel in 1 Kings 21:17–29?

And the word of the LORD came to Elijah the Tishbite, saying, Arise, go down to meet Ahab king of Israel, which is in Samaria: behold, he is in the vineyard of Naboth, whither he is gone down to possess it. And thou shalt speak unto him, saying, thus saith the LORD, Hast thou killed, and also taken possession? And thou shalt speak unto him, saying, Thus saith the LORD, in the place where dogs licked the blood of Naboth shall dogs lick thy blood, even thine. And Ahab said to Elijah, Hast thou find me , O mine enemy? And he answered, I have found thee: because thou hast sold thyself to work evil in the sight of the LORD. Behold, I will bring evil upon thee, and take away thy posterity, and will cut off from Ahab him that pisseth against the wall, and him that is shut up and left in Israel. And will make thine house like the house of Jeroboam the son of Nebat, and like the house of baasha the son of Ahijah, for the provocation wherewith thou hast provoked me to anger, and made Israel to sin, and of Jezebel also spake the LORD, saying, The dogs shall eat Jezebel by the wall of Jericho. Him that dieth of Ahab in the city the dogs shall eat; and him that dieth in the field shall the fowls of the air eat. But there was none like unto Ahab, which did sell himself to work wickedness in the sight of the LORD, whom jezebel his wife stirred up. And he did very abominably in following idols, according to all things as did the Amorites, whom the LORD cast out before the children of Israel. And it came to pass, when Ahab heard those words, that he rent his clothes, and put sackcloth upon his flesh, and fasted, and lay in sackcloth, and went softly. And the word of the LORD came to Elijah the Tishbite, saying. Seest thou how Ahab humbleth himself before me? Because Ahab humbleth himself before me, I will not bring the evil in his days; but in his son's days will I bring the evil upon his house.

There is nothing else on earth available to man that comes close to what prayer can do. Like Esther, do not sit in pity of yourself. Do not wait to point out what is wrong and complain about how God keeps silent and is not doing anything to change the situation. Do not sit and wait for the powers that be to help you. Do not wait for anointed ministers who are yet unborn. Take action and take it now. Do not wait. Engage the Lord in prayer and experience Him practically in power. Now read Esther 3–9 for more insight. I recommend that you read through these seven chapters in the book of Esther.

Barriers to Prayer

Now consider Psalm 66:16–20:

> Come and hear, all ye that fear God, and I will declare
> what he hath done for my soul. I cried unto him with my
> mouth, and he was extolled with my tongue. If I regard
> iniquity in my heart, the Lord will not hear me: But verily
> God hath heard me; he hath attended to the voice of my
> prayer. Blessed be God, which hath not turned away my
> prayer, nor his mercy from me.

The greatest barrier to prayer is sin. Sin is the only thing that can hinder you in prayer. God will not hear the prayer of the sinner. "Therefore they say unto God, Depart from us; for we desire not the knowledge of thy ways. What is the Almighty, that we should serve him? and what profit should we have, if we pray unto him?" (Job 21: 14–15).

How to Pray Heaven and Earth moving prayers

Consider 1 Kings 18: 41-46:

> And Elijah said unto Ahab, Get thee up, eat and
> drink; for there is a sound of abundance of rain. So Ahab
> went up to eat and to drink. And Elijah went up to the top
> of Carmel; and he cast himself down upon the earth, and
> put his face between his knees, And said to his servant,
> Go up now, look toward the sea. And he went up, and
> looked, and said, There is nothing. And he said, Go again
> seven times. And it came to pass at the seventh time, that
> he said, Behold, there ariseth a little cloud out of the sea,
> like a man's hand. And he said, Go up, say unto Ahab,
> Prepare thy chariot, and get thee down that the rain stop

thee not. And it came to pass in the meanwhile, that the heaven was black with clouds and wind, and there was a great rain. And Ahab rode, and went to Jezreel. And the hand of the LORD was on Elijah; and he girded up his loins, and ran before Ahab to the entrance of Jezreel.

For more insight, you can also read Acts 4:23–32, which says the following:

> And being let go, they went to their own company, and reported all that the chief priests and elders had said unto them. And when they heard that, they lifted up their voice to God with one accord, and said, Lord, thou art God, which hast made heaven, and earth, and the sea, and all that in them is: Who by the mouth of thy servant David hast said, Why did the heathen rage, and the people imagine vain things? The kings of the earth stood up, and the rulers were gathered together against the Lord, and against his Christ. For of a truth against thy holy child Jesus, whom thou hast anointed, both Herod, and Pontius Pilate, with the Gentiles, and the people of Israel, were gathered together, For to do whatsoever thy hand and thy counsel determined before to be done. And now, Lord, behold their threatenings: and grant unto thy servants, that with all boldness they may speak thy word, By stretching forth thine hand to heal; and that signs and wonders may be done by the name of thy holy child Jesus. And when they had prayed, the place was shaken where they were assembled together; and they were all filled with the Holy Ghost, and they spake the word of God with boldness. And the multitude of them that believed were of one heart and of one soul: neither said any of them that ought of the things which he possessed was his own; but they had all things common.

Prayer can move heaven and earth when we understand how to pray. In James 4:2–3, the Bible says, "Ye lust, and have not: ye kill, and desire to have, and cannot obtain: ye fight and war, yet ye have not, because ye ask not. Ye ask, and receive not, because ye ask amiss, that ye may consume it upon your lusts." We can see from the aforementioned scriptures that prayer goes beyond "whosoever that call upon the name of the LORD." This does not mean that scripture is not relevant. It is more than relevant, but for us to do greater works for God and His kingdom and not just for ourselves, we must understand how to pray effectively. When you study prayers in the Holy Bible, you will understand how the people of God prayed and why their prayers carried so much power. His greatness and His power, glory, victory, and majesty were revealed because mortals prayed. James also wrote in James 5:17, "Elias was a man subject to like passions as we are, and he prayed earnestly that it might not rain: and it rained not on the earth by the space of three years and six months." There are ways that we can pray to move the heavens and earth, and I would like to share some of them here. I have added some prayer points at the end of this book for those who want to take action in their prayer lives right away.

Prayer and Fasting

One of the most powerful ways you can pray is with fasting. Our Lord and Savior had said, "Howbeit this kind goeth not out but by prayer and fasting" (Matthew 17:21).

Adding fasting to prayer is the most effective way you can pray. When you want God to be involved in situations or circumstances, humble yourself with a fast before Him. When the mountains seem insurmountable, add fasting to your prayers. When it is a life-and-death situation, add fasting to your prayers. When it is a battle of the kingdoms, add fasting to your prayers. At the start of a ministry, add fasting to your prayers. When you sense that you are up against a wall, add fasting to your prayer. Fasting and prayer is the most lethal combination available against the Devil and his agency.

> Then Esther bade them return Mordecai this answer,
> Go, gather together all the Jews that are present in
> Shushan, and fast ye for me, and neither eat nor drink
> three days, night or day: I also and my maidens will fast
> likewise; and so will I go in unto the king, which is not
> according to the law: and if I perish, I perish. So Mordecai
> went his way, and did according to all that Esther had
> commanded him. (Esther 4:15–17)

If you have backslidden and fallen and you desire a restoration,
add fasting to your prayers. When you are praying for the seriously
sick person, add fasting to your prayers. When you are praying for
deliverance from demonic bondages, add fasting to your prayers.
Consider 2 Chronicles 20:1–13.

> It came to pass after this also, that the children of
> Moab, and the children of Ammon, and with them other
> beside the Ammonites, came against Jehoshaphat to battle.
> Then there came some that told Jehoshaphat, saying, There
> cometh a great multitude against thee from beyond the sea
> on this side Syria; and, behold, they be in Hazazontamar,
> which is Engedi. And Jehoshaphat feared, and set himself
> to seek the LORD, and proclaimed a fast throughout all
> Judah. And Judah gathered themselves together, to ask
> help of the LORD: even out of all the cities of Judah they
> came to seek the LORD. And Jehoshaphat stood in the
> congregation of Judah and Jerusalem, in the house of
> the LORD, before the new court, And said, O LORD God
> of our fathers, art not thou God in heaven? and rulest not
> thou over all the kingdoms of the heathen? and in thine
> hand is there not power and might, so that none is able
> to withstand thee? Art not thou our God, who didst drive
> out the inhabitants of this land before thy people Israel,
> and gavest it to the seed of Abraham thy friend for ever?

And they dwelt therein, and have built thee a sanctuary therein for thy name, saying, If, when evil cometh upon us, as the sword, judgment, or pestilence, or famine, we stand before this house, and in thy presence, (for thy name is in this house,) and cry unto thee in our affliction, then thou wilt hear and help. And now, behold, the children of Ammon and Moab and mount Seir, whom thou wouldest not let Israel invade, when they came out of the land of Egypt, but they turned from them, and destroyed them not; Behold, I say, how they reward us, to come to cast us out of thy possession, which thou hast given us to inherit. O our God, wilt thou not judge them? for we have no might against this great company that cometh against us; neither know we what to do: but our eyes are upon thee. And all Judah stood before the LORD, with their little ones, their wives, and their children.

Let's read through Matthew 17:14–21 together.

And when they were come to the multitude, there came to him a certain man, kneeling down to him, and saying, Lord, have mercy on my son: for he is lunatic, and sore vexed: for oftentimes he falleth into the fire, and oft into the water. And I brought him to thy disciples, and they could not cure him. Then Jesus answered and said, O faithless and perverse generation, how long shall I be with you? how long shall I suffer you? bring him hither to me. And Jesus rebuked the devil; and he departed out of him: and the child was cured from that very hour. Then came the disciples to Jesus apart, and said, Why could not we cast him out? And Jesus said unto them, Because of your unbelief: for verily I say unto you, If ye have faith as a grain of mustard seed, ye shall say unto this mountain, Remove hence to yonder place; and it shall remove; and nothing shall be impossible unto you. Howbeit this kind goeth not out but by prayer and fasting.

Fasting and praying has proven to be the most effective way to pray. Throughout the Holy Scripture, individuals like Daniel, Jacob, and David and even the entire nation of Israel pulled themselves from the brink of destruction through the powerful combination of prayer and fasting. You, too, can move heaven and earth by adding fasting to prayers. There are several types of fasts you can try, but I respectfully recommend only a few.

Take Ezra 8:21–3, for example. "Then I proclaimed a fast there, at the river of Ahava, that we might afflict ourselves before our God, to seek of him a right way for us, and for our little ones, and for all our substance. For I was ashamed to require of the king a band of soldiers and horsemen to help us against the enemy in the way: because we had spoken unto the king, saying, The hand of our God is upon all them for good that seek him; but his power and his wrath is against all them that forsake him."

Or consider Esther 4:15–17: "Then Esther bade them return Mordecai this answer, Go, gather together all the Jews that are present in Shushan, and fast ye for me, and neither eat nor drink three days, night or day: I also and my maidens will fast likewise; and so will I go in unto the king, which is not according to the law: and if I perish, I perish. So Mordecai went his way, and did according to all that Esther had commanded him."

You may consider a three- or seven-day dry fast without food, drinks, or even fruits. But, if you have a medical issue, first consult with your doctors before youe engage on any fast. When you undergo this kind of fast,break it lightly with warm drinks like tea, hot chocolate, or warm water. (Never break a long dry fast with cold drinks or hard food.) Then you can steadily add solid food a little at a time every few hours. Read this prayer of Nehemiah 1:1–11:

The words of Nehemiah the son of Hachaliah. And it came to pass in the month Chisleu, in the twentieth year, as I was in Shushan the palace, That Hanani, one of my brethren, came, he and certain men of Judah; and I asked them concerning the Jews that had escaped, which were left of the captivity, and concerning Jerusalem. And they said unto me, The remnant that are left of the captivity there in the province are in great affliction and reproach: the wall of Jerusalem also is broken down, and the gates thereof are burned with fire. And it came to pass, when I heard these words, that I sat down and wept, and mourned certain days, and fasted, and prayed before the God of heaven, And said, I beseech thee, O LORD God of heaven, the great and terrible God, that keepeth covenant and mercy for them that love him and observe his commandments: Let thine ear now be attentive, and thine eyes open, that thou mayest hear the prayer of thy servant, which I pray before thee now, day and night, for the children of Israel thy servants, and confess the sins of the children of Israel, which we have sinned against thee: both I and my father's house have sinned. We have dealt very corruptly against thee, and have not kept thy commandments, nor thy statutes, nor the judgments, which thou commandedst thy servant Moses. Remember, I beseech thee, the word that thou commandedst thy servant Moses, saying, If ye transgress, I will scatter you abroad among the nations: But if ye turn unto me, and keep my commandments, and do them; though there were of you cast out unto the uttermost part of the heaven, yet will I gather them from thence, and will bring them unto the place that I have chosen to set my name there. Now these are thy servants and thy people, whom thou hast redeemed by thy great power, and by thy strong hand. O LORD, I beseech thee, let now thine ear be attentive to the prayer of thy servant, and to the prayer of thy servants, who desire to fear thy name: and prosper, I pray thee, thy servant this day, and grant him mercy in the sight of this man. For I was the king's cupbearer.

Praying At The Midnight Hours (between 12:00.a.m. and 3.00 a.m).

"Another parable put he forth unto them, saying, The kingdom of heaven is likened unto a man which sowed good seed in his field: But while men slept, his enemy came and sowed tares among the wheat, and went his way. But when the blade was sprung up, and brought forth fruit, then appeared the tares also. So the servants of the householder came and said unto him, Sir, didst not thou sow good seed in thy field? from whence then hath it tares?

He said unto them, An enemy hath done this. The servants said unto him, Wilt thou then that we go and gather them up?" (Matthew 13:24–28).

From this parable, we can deduce that most of the wickedness of the enemy is done when men are sleeping at night. The Devil knows that the best time to attack is when his target is unaware, weak, and vulnerable. Therefore, when you pray regularly at the midnight hours, you leave the Devil no room for attack. Rather, you are the one on the offensive, and the Devil is on the defensive. From the previous passages, we can see that most of the work of the enemy is finished while we are asleep and that we wake to see the manifestation of this work. Midnight prayers will leave the enemy virtually no room for attack. You will always be one step ahead of the enemy when you regularly pray at the midnight hour. I understand that it can be very difficult for most people, but if you want results badly, you work for them.

Midnight praying is so effective in deliverance because if you pray deliverance prayers during the day and go to sleep at night, you are opening up yourself for attacks. The enemy will fight back when they are most effective, the midnight hour. Because the spirits of darkness most of the times need your consent and wants you to be as vulnerable as possible for them to inflict the most harm.

Pray Until Something Happens (Operation PUSH)

One should pray until something happens (Operation PUSH). You can make your prayers very effective and powerful if you pray for a long time and you are determined not to take no for an answer. Consider Daniel 10:1–14, which says the following:

> In the third year of Cyrus king of Persia a thing was revealed unto Daniel, whose name was called Belteshazzar; and the thing was true, but the time appointed was long: and he understood the thing, and had understanding of the vision. In those days I Daniel was mourning three full weeks. I ate no pleasant bread, neither came flesh nor wine in my mouth, neither did I anoint myself at all, till three whole weeks were fulfilled. And in the four and twentieth day of the first month, as I was by the side of the great river, which is Hiddekel; Then I lifted up mine eyes, and looked, and behold a certain man clothed in linen, whose loins were girded with fine gold of Uphaz: His body also was like the beryl, and his face as the appearance of lightning, and his eyes as lamps of fire, and his arms and his feet like in colour to polished brass, and the voice of his words like the voice of a multitude. And I Daniel alone saw the vision: for the men that were with me saw not the vision; but a great quaking fell upon them, so that they fled to hide themselves. Therefore I was left alone, and saw this great vision, and there remained no strength in me: for my comeliness was turned in me into corruption, and I retained no strength. Yet heard I the voice of his words: and when I heard the voice of his words, then was I in a deep sleep on my face, and my face toward the ground. And, behold, an hand touched me, which set me upon my knees and upon the palms of my hands. And he said unto me, O Daniel, a

man greatly beloved, understand the words that I speak unto thee, and stand upright: for unto thee am I now sent. And when he had spoken this word unto me, I stood trembling. Then said he unto me, Fear not, Daniel: for from the first day that thou didst set thine heart to understand, and to chasten thyself before thy God, thy words were heard, and I am come for thy words. But the prince of the kingdom of Persia withstood me one and twenty days: but, lo, Michael, one of the chief princes, came to help me; and I remained there with the kings of Persia. Now I am come to make thee understand what shall befall thy people in the latter days: for yet the vision is for many days.

In 1 Samuel 1:1–18, we see how Hannah stepped out and over all that was weighing her down, over her mate's insults, over her husband's sympathy, which only tended to worsen her situation, and above all, over the ungodly condemnation of her by Eli, the high priest, and his evil pronouncement. She did so to engage God Almighty directly through prayer. Eli was the high priest of the day, the supposed oracle of God at the moment, but because of the actions of his sons against God and His people, he was no longer engaged in living relationship with God. Hence, he could not perceive the bitterness of Hannah's soul. Rather, he imagined that she was drunk to be doing what she was doing (seemingly talking to herself). Because of her faith to call upon GOD in these situations: A situation were her loving, caring husband could only sympathize with her; a situation were the most religious person of her day did nothing but rather only provoked her and tried to make the situation worse, before turning around to pronounce the following blessing on her: "Then Eli answered and said, Go in peace: and the God of Israel grant thee thy petition that thou hast asked of him" (1 Samuel 1:17).

This blessing from Eli from the aforementioned scripture, I

believe, was in response to her prayer, which God had already heard before the rude intrusion by the high priest. And the rest of the response to her prayer played out so vividly. She became pregnant thereafter and gave birth to a boy who eventually became the greatest judge, priest, and prophet of Israel.

Are you surrounded by the most impossible and most insurmountable situations in your life right now? The only plausible thing you can do is pray just like Hannah did. Do not feed on the insults, humiliations, and condemnations of the religious powers of today or the sympathy of love ones. Only you can rise above everything around you and engage God through the oracle of prayer. You can go to God personally through prayer. He says this in Matthew 21:22. "And all things, whatsoever ye shall ask in prayer, believing, ye shall receive."

There are so many people who do not pray except when they are in a church. Some need the motivation of others, and many believe that they can only receive their hearts' desires if a more righteous person prays for them. This is a lie of the Devil, and it has robbed so many of the power of prayer. While all these may be good to some extent, the oracle of prayer is more effective when every individual engages in prayer themselves. Then you can go before Him alone, and He can easily impact you with His glory. You can make your request more clearly as it affects you personally. When you engage the oracle of prayer, you are there with God. There are not any distractions, no unspoken competitions. You rise above doubt and fear and enter into the most powerful place of faith, knowing your heavenly Father is with you and listening with undivided attention to every one of your complaints and requests. Read what happen when Hezekiah engage the oracle of prayer in Isaiah 38:1–8.

> In those days was Hezekiah sick unto death. And Isaiah the prophet the son of Amoz came unto him, and said unto him, Thus saith the LORD, Set thine house in

order: for thou shalt die, and not live. Then Hezekiah turned his face toward the wall, and prayed unto the LORD, And said, Remember now, O LORD, I beseech thee, how I have walked before thee in truth and with a perfect heart, and have done that which is good in thy sight. And Hezekiah wept sore. Then came the word of the LORD to Isaiah, saying, Go, and say to Hezekiah, Thus saith the LORD, the God of David thy father, I have heard thy prayer, I have seen thy tears: behold, I will add unto thy days fifteen years. And I will deliver thee and this city out of the hand of the king of Assyria: and I will defend this city. And this shall be a sign unto thee from the LORD, that the LORD will do this thing that he hath spoken; Behold, I will bring again the shadow of the degrees, which is gone down in the sun dial of Ahaz, ten degrees backward. So the sun returned ten degrees, by which degrees it was gone down.

This is powerful. Hezekiah could have held onto the prophet Isaiah's cloak and wept and begged the most powerful man of God to pray for him, thereby accepting the message from the man of God. He would have wasted precious time. The man of GOD could have said either of the following: "God has spoken. I cannot change it." Or, "If the Lord says something otherwise, I will let you know, but for now, this is all I have." No, he refused the message and engaged the oracle of prayer where there is no middleman; you are alone with the almighty God, one on one. We are closest to God when we are praying. And so the Lord did not have to change His mind as many will think. He answered Hezekiah's prayer, which is what the Bible says in Matthew 21:22, "And all things, whatsoever ye shall ask in prayer, believing, ye shall receive." There is a lesson to learn here. The Devil is the one that afflicted Hezekiah with a sickness bad enough to cause death, but through the oracle of prayer, God was called into the situation. Are you facing a situation like sickness, debt, lack, poverty, disfavor, marital failure, abuse, addiction, etc.? When you engage the oracle of prayer, God comes into the equation, and everything else melts away.

This is what I call "the Hezekiah Situation": Sickness will cause death or suffering. But Hezekiah will not accept any of these;

Consider the following Situations:

Hezekiah decided to bring the Lord into his situation through the oracle of prayer and received a different outcome from what was eminent; suffering and ultimately death. Rather, the inevitable was avoided, his health was restored and fifteen years was added to his life. I don't know what your situation look like right now, but if you are willing you can engage the Lord God almighty through His oracle: Prayer.

When you engage the oracle of prayer personally, your sins cannot hide. They will come to the surface, and then with humility, you can confess them and repent. I believe one of the reasons so many people are afraid to personally engage God in prayer is that they know their sins and want to continue in them for whatever reason. When they pray, those sins, cry out, and drown out any reasonable thing they want to say to the Lord, their minds become so noisy that they easily blank out, not remembering what they wanted to say in the first place. Others have never been taught the arts of praying because of denominational doctrines or leaders who themselves have failed to understand prayer. Having said that, I would like to emphasize that the oracle of prayer is one of the greatest, most powerful oracles of God that you can engage to resolve issues beyond your control and beyond the control of others (man).

From the most basic things of daily needs to the expansion of the kingdom of God here on earth to eternal life with Him in glory, all can be ordered right here and now by those who would endeavor to engage the oracle of prayer. Like God, its power is limitless, and its reach is without end. Its grace is unfathomable and incomprehensible, and its speed is light-years faster than the speed of light. "And it shall come to pass, that before they call, I will answer; and while they are yet speaking, I will hear" (Isaiah 65:24). Do not take my word for it. Take the twenty-one-day prayer and fasting challenge at the end of this book and convince yourself of the power of the oracle of prayer. And when you convince yourself, tell someone else and never cease from praying in Jesus' name. Amen.

Chapter 4

THE ORACLE OF SELFLESS SERVICE

He openeth also their ear to discipline and commandeth that they return from iniquity. If they obey and serve him they shall spend their days in prosperity and their years in pleasure.
Job 36:10–11

Now therefore, if ye will obey my voice indeed, and keep my covenant, then ye shall be a peculiar treasure unto me above all people: for all the earth is mine: And ye shall be unto me a kingdom of priests, and an holy nation. These are the words which thou shalt speak unto the children of Israel.
—Exodus 19:5–6.

But ye are a chosen generation, a royal priesthood, an holy nation, a peculiar people; that ye should shew forth the praises of him who hath called you out of darkness into his marvelous light; Which in time past were not a people, but are now the people of God: which had not obtained mercy, but now have obtained mercy.
—1 Peter 2:9–10

There is a story out of some churches in China that says that the members of the congregation welcome new believers by saying the following: "Jesus now has a new pair of eyes to see with, new ears to listen with, new hands to help with, and a new heart to love others with." This is the core of selfless service. We are united with Him, and we are one with Him. The fact that we are created and called to serve Him is very clear in the Holy Scripture. "And ye shall serve the LORD your God, and he shall bless thy bread, and thy water; and I will take sickness away from the midst of thee" (Exodus 23:25). The Bible also says in Jeremiah 1:5, "Before I formed thee in the belly I knew thee; and before thou camest forth out of the womb I sanctified thee, and I ordained thee a prophet unto the nations." In 1 Corinthians 3:5, it says, "Who then is Paul, and who is Apollos, but ministers by whom ye believed, even as the Lord gave to every man?" And in 2 Timothy 1:9, the Word of God say, "Who hath saved us, and called us with an holy calling, not according to our works, but according to his own purpose and grace, which was given us in Christ Jesus before the world began."

These are just a few passages that point to this truth. Our divine purpose on earth is to serve the Lord selflessly. We are supposed to show His praise and extend His salvation and good will to all mankind. The purpose of this chapter is to help us to see how God works through men to accomplish great things. Those who were of use to God recognized His purpose and made themselves available so that His divine ability, which has been given to each of us even before the foundation of the earth, could come into full effect to produce the results that the Lord had always intended. In other words, God's greatness, power, glory, victory, and majesty comes into play whenever someone steps out to serve in accordance to His divine purpose. Whenever someone answers the call to service, the power of God is brought to life to do great things.

What made Abraham, Moses, David, Elijah, Isaiah, Jeremiah, Ezekiel, Ezra, Nehemiah, Peter, and Paul such great oracles of God? It wasn't their prosperity, royal upbringing, strength, gifts, position, personality, humility, understanding, knowledge, experience, or scholarly achievement, respectively . All these may have help them down the road, but these were in no way what made them great. What made them great was their willingness to service and to serve selflessly. That was evident the moment Abraham answered God's call to raise a people unto Himself, a nation to be called after God. God's presence was with him every step of the way in fulfilling that call. Abraham was not a perfect man, but when it came to trusting God about His promise, he was perfect.

> After these things the word of the LORD came unto Abram in a vision, saying, Fear not, Abram: I am thy shield, and thy exceeding great reward. And Abram said, LORD God, what wilt thou give me, seeing I go childless, and the steward of my house is this Eliezer of Damascus? And Abram said, Behold, to me thou hast given no seed: and, lo, one born in my house is mine heir. And, behold, the word of the LORD came unto him, saying, This shall not be thine heir; but he that shall come forth out of thine own bowels shall be thine heir. And he brought him forth abroad, and said, Look now toward heaven, and tell the stars, if thou be able to number them: and he said unto him, So shall thy seed be. And he believed in the LORD; and he counted it to him for righteousness. (Genesis 15:1–6)

Now consider Romans 4:17–22:

> As it is written, I have made thee a father of many nations,) before him whom he believed, even God, who quickeneth the dead, and calleth those things which be not as though they were. Who against hope believed in hope, that he might become the father of many nations, according to that which was spoken, So shall thy seed be. And being not weak in faith, he considered not his own body now dead, when he was about an hundred

77

years old, neither yet the deadness of Sarah's womb: He staggered not at the promise of God through unbelief; but was strong in faith, giving glory to God; And being fully persuaded that, what he had promised, he was able also to perform. And therefore it was imputed to him for righteousness.

Because he trusted God, he waited patiently for the fulfillment of the promise, and the Lord worked through him to bring the promise to pass. He guided him through every derailment, frustration, and all the attempts by external forces to derail the divine purpose. God restored Sarah to him from those mightier than he was, and he defeated the raiding invaders of his day.

The apostle Paul became the greatest apostle, though some may argue that he was forced into that role by the events that happened on the road to Damacus. Yet, Paul willingly gave himself to that work and God's power shaped his service through mighty signs and miracles so that he could dismantle seemingly insurmountable oppositions. Are you drawn to healing the sick, building churches, casting out demons, taking the gospel to the unreached, or supporting the church? The power of God is available to pave the way, though you may encounter severe opposition or a lack of resources to begin; however, if you step out willingly to serve the Lord selflessly, the power of God will be ever-present to accomplish impossible things.

Most of the time, nobody knows how far or how great God will move until we step out of our comfort zones for selfless service.

Denying the Power of Selfless Service

The knowledge of God is paramount, and it is a prerequisite for an effective service. Prayer is also necessary. If you deny yourself any one of these, no matter how much you want to serve the Lord, your zeal will end in stillbirth. In other words, when you are without knowledge of the Lord and you are not prayerful, there will be no appetite for service (if you genuinely want to serve the Lord). The motivation will not be there. This is why being rich in the Word of God and being prayerful are the prerequisite oracles before the oracle of selfless service can be realized. In reality, those that deny the power of selfless service (service) are the ones the Bible describe in the following scripture; "Therefore they say unto God, Depart from us; for we desire not the knowledge of thy ways. What is the Almighty, that we should serve him? and what profit should we have, if we pray unto him?" (Job 21:14–15).

If the Word of God is too difficult for you to understand and prayer is too hard, you will lose the opportunity to serve God effectively. At best, you will be stuck in one dead-end church or another, serving a dead-end cause. The one place you can almost practically see God holding your hand to touch other people in their circumstances is in selfless service.Where through your service lives are being transformed and eminent disaster are turned around for victory, because you made yourself available and minister to those who need the Lord's message. Where the purpose of God is recognizable and the people feel inadequate or limited, waiting for the power of God to fall from heaven or an anointed servant of God to show up to lead, they might wait forever. The Bible says in 2Timothy 3:5, "Having a form of godliness, but denying the power thereof: from such turn away."

But when someone or a group of individuals are willing to step out as Ezra did.

> This Ezra went up from Babylon; and he was a ready scribe in the Law of Moses, which the LORD God of Israel had given: and the king granted him all his request, according to the hand of the LORD his God upon him. And there went up some of the children of Israel, and of the priests, and the Levites, and the singers, and the porters, and the Nethinims, unto Jerusalem, in the seventh year of Artaxerxes the king. And he came to Jerusalem in the

> fifth month, which was in the seventh year of the king.
> For upon the first day of the first month began he to go
> up from Babylon, and on the first day of the fifth month
> came he to Jerusalem, according to the good hand of his
> God upon him. For Ezra had prepared his heart to seek
> the law of the LORD, and to do it, and to teach in Israel
> statutes and judgments. (Ezra 7:6–10)

That selfless service or willingness to serve becomes the conduit
for God's power to bring that purpose to accomplishment. There
are so many people sitting on God's powers, waiting for someone to
come and take the lead, while God is saying to them, "Just step out.
I am waiting for you to just step out, and my power will come into
full effect."

The oracle of selfless service is the most practical; someone's
ministration (service) having a supernatural effect, to bring the
salvation, healing, deliverance, blessings and the knowledge of God
to a person or a people in need of Him. The oracles of God's Word
and prayer must have been harnessed well for the oracle of selfless
service to be effective.

The book of Job rightly captures this idea.

> Acquaint now thyself with him, and be at peace:
> thereby good shall come unto thee. Receive, I pray thee,
> the law from his mouth, and lay up his words in thine
> heart. If thou return to the Almighty, thou shalt be built
> up, thou shalt put away iniquity far from thy tabernacles.
> Then shalt thou lay up gold as dust, and the gold of Ophir
> as the stones of the brooks. Yea, the Almighty shall be
> thy defence, and thou shalt have plenty of silver. For then
> shalt thou have thy delight in the Almighty, and shalt lift
> up thy face unto God. Thou shalt make thy prayer unto
> him, and he shall hear thee, and thou shalt pay thy vows.
> Thou shalt also decree a thing, and it shall be established

unto thee: and the light shall shine upon thy ways. When men are cast down, then thou shalt say, There is lifting up; and he shall save the humble person. He shall deliver the island of the innocent: and it is delivered by the pureness of thine hands. (Job 22:21–30). From the foregoing scripture we can see the benefits of knowing Him, staying connected to Him at all times and seeking always to better this knowledge. The promise of answered prayer as motivation

The Reward

The Word of the Lord is very clear about how God will reward those who do His will and the people who are willing to step out to serve His purpose, whether it's popular or not, whether the odds are against you or not. He told Abraham the following in Genesis 12:1–3.

> Now the LORD had said unto Abram, Get thee out of thy country, and from thy kindred, and from thy father's house, unto a land that I will shew thee: And I will make of thee a great nation, and I will bless thee, and make thy name great; and thou shalt be a blessing: And I will bless them that bless thee, and curse him that curseth thee: and in thee shall all families of the earth be blessed.

Now consider Genesis 13:2: "And Abram was very rich in cattle, in silver, and in gold." And what about Genesis 15:1? "After these things the word of the LORD came unto Abram in a vision, saying, Fear not, Abram: I am thy shield, and thy exceeding great reward."

Joseph served his master so faithfully that the master left all of his possessions and estates in Joseph's care, and because of that trust, the Lord blessed him so greatly.

> And Joseph was brought down to Egypt; and Potiphar, an officer of Pharaoh, captain of the guard, an Egyptian, bought him of the hands of the Ishmeelites, which had brought him down thither. And the LORD was with Joseph, and he was a prosperous man; and he was in the house of his master the Egyptian. And his master saw that the LORD was with him, and that the LORD made all that he did to prosper in his hand. And Joseph found grace in his sight, and he served him: and he made him overseer over his house, and all that he had he put into his hand. And it came to pass from the time that he had made him overseer in his house, and over all that he had, that the LORD blessed the Egyptian's house for Joseph's sake; and the blessing of the LORD was upon all that he had in the house, and in the field. And he left all that he had in Joseph's hand; and he knew not ought he had, save the bread which he did eat. And Joseph was a goodly person, and well favoured. (Genesis 39:1–6)

And even after he received a false accusation from his master's wife and he was unjustly punished and thrown into prison, he did not begrudge his accuser. He didn't fall into depression from self-pity. Rather, he continued to do well in the prison, and the Lord again was there with him.

> But the LORD was with Joseph, and shewed him mercy, and gave him favour in the sight of the keeper of the prison. And the keeper of the prison committed to Joseph's hand all the prisoners that were in the prison; and whatsoever they did there, he was the doer of it. The keeper of the prison looked not to anything that was under his hand; because the LORD was with him, and that which he did, the LORD made it to prosper. (Genesis 39:21–3)

Even after Pharaoh's butler forgot about Joseph and could not do anything to help him, when God wanted the butler to remember Joseph, he did. Then the reward for his diligent service came in such a powerful way that no man and no force of darkness could reverse it because whatever God does is forever and ever. "I know that, whatsoever God doeth, it shall be forever: nothing can be put to it, nor any thing taken from it: and God doeth it, that men should fear before him" (Ecclesiastes 3:14).

Because he was faithful even in such a strange and hostile environment, the power of God worked out His eternal purpose every step of the way, even through hard and impossible situations (been a stranger, a slave and a convict), to ultimately save that generation through the hand of Joseph. Consider Genesis 41:37–57, which says the following:

> And the thing was good in the eyes of Pharaoh, and in the eyes of all his servants. And Pharaoh said unto his servants, Can we find such a one as this is, a man in whom the Spirit of God is? And Pharaoh said unto Joseph, Forasmuch as God hath shewed thee all this, there is none so discreet and wise as thou art: Thou shalt be over my house, and according unto thy word shall all my people be ruled: only in the throne will I be greater than thou. And Pharaoh said unto Joseph, See, I have set thee over all the land of Egypt. And Pharaoh took off his ring from his hand, and put it upon Joseph's hand, and arrayed him in vestures of fine linen, and put a gold chain about his neck; And he made him to ride in the second chariot which he had; and they cried before him, Bow the knee: and he made him ruler over all the land of Egypt. And Pharaoh said unto Joseph, I am Pharaoh, and without thee shall no man lift up his hand or foot in all the land of Egypt. And Pharaoh called Joseph's name Zaphnathpaaneah; and he gave him to wife Asenath the

daughter of Potipherah priest of On. And Joseph went out over all the land of Egypt. And Joseph was thirty years old when he stood before Pharaoh king of Egypt. And Joseph went out from the presence of Pharaoh, and went throughout all the land of Egypt. And in the seven plenteous years the earth brought forth by handfuls. And he gathered up all the food of the seven years, which were in the land of Egypt, and laid up the food in the cities: the food of the field, which was round about every city, laid he up in the same. And Joseph gathered corn as the sand of the sea, very much, until he left numbering; for it was without number. And unto Joseph were born two sons before the years of famine came, which Asenath the daughter of Potipherah priest of On bare unto him. And Joseph called the name of the firstborn Manasseh: For God, said he, hath made me forget all my toil, and all my father's house. And the name of the second called he Ephraim: For God hath caused me to be fruitful in the land of my affliction. And the seven years of plenteousness, that was in the land of Egypt, were ended. And the seven years of dearth began to come, according as Joseph had said: and the dearth was in all lands; but in all the land of Egypt there was bread. And when all the land of Egypt was famished, the people cried to Pharaoh for bread: and Pharaoh said unto all the Egyptians, Go unto Joseph; what he saith to you, do. And the famine was over all the face of the earth: and Joseph opened all the storehouses, and sold unto the Egyptians; and the famine waxed sore in the land of Egypt. And all countries came into Egypt to Joseph for to buy corn; because that the famine was so sore in all lands.

Moses risked his life and went back to Egypt to deliver the children of Israel from bondage. Thus, the Lord had to promote him over his enemy, the king of Egypt, by making him a "god". "And the LORD said unto Moses, See, I have made thee a god to Pharaoh: and Aaron thy brother shall be thy prophet" (Exodus 7:1).

God will promote you over your opposition so that you may prevail and reign over them. The Lord has to raise Moses to the status of a "god" above the pharaoh-god inoder to subdue him. This was how the Holy Scripture concluded the story of Moses in his selfless service unto the Lord God:

> And Joshua the son of Nun was full of the spirit of wisdom; for Moses had laid his hands upon him: and the children of Israel hearkened unto him, and did as the LORD commanded Moses. And there arose not a prophet since in Israel like unto Moses, whom the LORD knew face-to-face, In all the signs and the wonders, which the LORD sent him to do in the land of Egypt to Pharaoh, and to all his servants, and to all his land, and in all that mighty hand, and in all the great terror which Moses shewed in the sight of all Israel. (Deuteronomy 34:9–12)

Samuel, who served the people of Israel as judge, prophet, and priest, had these accolades in 1 Samuel 12.

> And Samuel said unto all Israel, Behold, I have hearkened unto your voice in all that ye said unto me, and have made a king over you. And now, behold, the king walketh before you: and I am old and gray-headed; and, behold, my sons are with you: and I have walked before you from my childhood unto this day. Behold, here I am: witness against me before the LORD, and before his anointed: whose ox have I taken? or whose ass have I taken? or whom have I defrauded? whom have I oppressed? or of whose hand have I received any bribe to blind mine eyes therewith? and I will restore it you. And

they said, Thou hast not defrauded us, nor oppressed us, neither hast thou taken ought of any man's hand. And he said unto them, The LORD is witness against you, and his anointed is witness this day, that ye have not found ought in my hand. And they answered, He is witness. And Samuel said unto the people, It is the LORD that advanced Moses and Aaron, and that brought your fathers up out of the land of Egypt. Now therefore stand still, that I may reason with you before the LORD of all the righteous acts of the LORD, which he did to you and to your fathers. When Jacob was come into Egypt, and your fathers cried unto the LORD, then the LORD sent Moses and Aaron, which brought forth your fathers out of Egypt, and made them dwell in this place. And when they forgat the LORD their God, he sold them into the hand of Sisera, captain of the host of Hazor, and into the hand of the Philistines, and into the hand of the king of Moab, and they fought against them. And they cried unto the LORD, and said, We have sinned, because we have forsaken the LORD, and have served Baalim and Ashtaroth: but now deliver us out of the hand of our enemies, and we will serve thee. And the LORD sent Jerubbaal, and Bedan, and Jephthah, and Samuel, and delivered you out of the hand of your enemies on every side, and ye dwelled safe. And when ye saw that Nahash the king of the children of Ammon came against you, ye said unto me, Nay; but a king shall reign over us: when the LORD your God was your king. Now therefore behold the king whom ye have chosen, and whom ye have desired! and, behold, the LORD hath set a king over you. If ye will fear the LORD, and serve him, and obey his voice, and not rebel against the commandment of the LORD, then shall both ye and also the king that reigneth over you continue following the LORD your God: But if ye will not obey the voice of the LORD, but rebel against the commandment of the LORD, then shall the hand of the LORD be against you, as it was against your fathers. Now therefore stand and see this great thing, which the LORD will do before your eyes. Is it not wheat harvest to day? I will call unto the LORD, and he shall send thunder and rain; that ye may perceive and see that your wickedness is great, which ye have done in the sight of the LORD, in asking you a king. So Samuel called unto the LORD; and the LORD sent thunder and rain that day: and all the people greatly feared the LORD and Samuel. And all the people said unto Samuel, Pray for thy servants unto the LORD thy God, that we die not: for we have added unto all our sins this evil, to ask us a king. And Samuel said unto the people, Fear not: ye have done all this wickedness: yet turn not aside from following the LORD, but serve the LORD with all your heart; And turn ye not aside: for then should ye go after vain things, which cannot profit nor deliver; for they are vain. For the LORD will not forsake his people for his great name's sake: because it hath pleased the LORD to make you his people. Moreover as for me, God forbid that I should sin against the LORD in ceasing to pray for you: but I will teach you the good and the right way: Only fear the LORD, and serve him in truth with all your heart: for consider how great things he hath done for you. But if ye shall still do wickedly, ye shall be consumed, both ye and your king.

Also, consider 1 Samuel 25:1 "And Samuel died; and all the Israelites were gathered together, and lamented him, and buried him in his house at Ramah. And David arose, and went down to the wilderness of Paran."

He was so successful in his service to his people. He was perfect and blameless. Meanwhile, our Lord and Savior has promised us even greater rewards in this our dispensation, as it is written in Matthew 19:27–30.

> Then answered Peter and said unto him, Behold, we have forsaken all, and followed thee; what shall we have therefore? And Jesus said unto them, Verily I say unto you, That ye which have followed me, in the regeneration when the Son of man shall sit in the throne of his glory, ye also shall sit upon twelve thrones, judging the twelve tribes of Israel. And every one that hath forsaken houses, or brethren, or sisters, or father, or mother, or wife, or children, or lands, for my name's sake, shall receive an hundredfold, and shall inherit everlasting life. But many that are first shall be last; and the last shall be first.

And how about Mark 10:28–31?

> Then Peter began to say unto him, Lo, we have left all, and have followed thee. And Jesus answered and said, Verily I say unto you, There is no man that hath left house, or brethren, or sisters, or father, or mother, or wife, or children, or lands, for my sake, and the gospel's, But he shall receive an hundredfold now in this time, houses, and brethren, and sisters, and mothers, and children, and lands, with persecutions; and in the world to come eternal life. But many that are first shall be last; and the last first.

Finally, read over Mark 16:14–18.

> Afterward he appeared unto the eleven as they sat at meat, and upbraided them with their unbelief and

hardness of heart, because they believed not them which had seen him after he was risen. And he said unto them, Go ye into all the world, and preach the gospel to every creature. He that believeth and is baptized shall be saved; but he that believeth not shall be damned. And these signs shall follow them that believe; In my name shall they cast out devils; they shall speak with new tongues; They shall take up serpents; and if they drink any deadly thing, it shall not hurt them; they shall lay hands on the sick, and they shall recover.

In the recent past, we have heard about the labor of love of Evans Roberts, who cried unto God day and night, "Give me Wales, or I die." And because of his selfless service, one of the greatest revival of the early twentieth century broke out, one that affected the entire people of Wales as well as animals. Furthermore, from a little village in Nigeria, people have reported about how the power of God broke forth to heal the sick people. There was an epidemic of cholera in the entire village. There were no medical facilities or solutions, and people were dying by the hour. A young man who had been newly converted decided to do something about it. He went over to the well, the only source of drinking water in the village, prayed over the water, drew out some, and sent it to all who were sick. Everyone who drank the water recovered, and that was the end of the cholera outbreak in that village.

Your gift is your link with God. When you draw on that link, whether through an act of kindness, a work of faith, an expression of love, or an intervention, God's glory and might is revealed. God Almighty is calling out for His gifts in you, and if only you can draw on them, He will release Himself from the other end.

The gift of God is a spark of Him hidden within us, waiting to be uncovered. You can tap into this spark and draw on it for the miraculous power of God to aid you. Though the gift may reveal itself in mediums as crude as dreams or as salient as wisdom, once you can draw on it, it releases the very essence of God when it is used for the good of others and mankind in general. This is what I call selfless service.

Selfless service is divinely powerful because you are in agreement with God, working together with Him from two different ends—God working from the supernatural and you in the natural to accomplish something good for others. "I can do all things through Christ which strengtheneth me" (Philippians 4:13).

Whenever we apply our divine gifts for the good of others, whether the benefits are revealed in the small things of everyday life or huge miraculous life events, selfless service is at the very heart of God. There is nothing in life that is more divinely and more naturally rewarding than when people step in to accomplish what is already in the heart of God, doing so for the glory of GOD and the good of mankind.

The oracle of selfless service is by far the most revealing of the powers of God and His heart. When men step out even in the simplest ways, they end up looking as though they have divine powers. This is what God intended from the foundation of the earth, and this is why every other thing that God has ever done on earth (apart from creation) has been done through acts of selfless service. Consider the righteous Abel or Jesus, who made the ultimate sacrifice for the salvation of mankind. Think about the apostle John in the book of Revelation, who received prophecies through relentless prayer and fasting. "And God said, Let us make man in our image, after our likeness: and let them have dominion over the fish of the sea, and over the fowl of the air, and over the cattle, and over all the earth, and over every creeping thing that creepeth upon the earth" (Genesis 1:26).

For this case studies, read through Genesis 40.

> And it came to pass after these things, that the butler
> of the king of Egypt and his baker had offended their lord

the king of Egypt. And Pharaoh was wroth against two of his officers, against the chief of the butlers, and against the chief of the bakers. And he put them in ward in the house of the captain of the guard, into the prison, the place where Joseph was bound. And the captain of the guard charged Joseph with them, and he served them: and they continued a season in ward. And they dreamed a dream both of them, each man his dream in one night, each man according to the interpretation of his dream, the butler and the baker of the king of Egypt, which were bound in the prison. And Joseph came in unto them in the morning, and looked upon them, and, behold, they were sad. And he asked Pharaoh's officers that were with him in the ward of his lord's house, saying, Wherefore look ye so sadly to day? And they said unto him, We have dreamed a dream, and there is no interpreter of it. And Joseph said unto them, Do not interpretations belong to God? tell me them, I pray you. And the chief butler told his dream to Joseph, and said to him, In my dream, behold, a vine was before me; And in the vine were three branches: and it was as though it budded, and her blossoms shot forth; and the clusters thereof brought forth ripe grapes: And Pharaoh's cup was in my hand: and I took the grapes, and pressed them into Pharaoh's cup, and I gave the cup into Pharaoh's hand. And Joseph said unto him, This is the interpretation of it: The three branches are three days: Yet within three days shall Pharaoh lift up thine head, and restore thee unto thy place: and thou shalt deliver Pharaoh's cup into his hand, after the former manner when thou wast his butler. But think on me when it shall be well with thee, and shew kindness, I pray thee, unto me, and make mention of me unto Pharaoh, and bring me out of this house: For indeed I was stolen away out of the land of the Hebrews: and here also have I done nothing that they should put me into the dungeon. When the chief baker saw that the interpretation was good, he said unto Joseph, I also was in my dream, and, behold, I had three white baskets on my head: And in the uppermost basket there was of all manner of bakemeats for Pharaoh; and the birds did eat them out of the basket upon my head. And Joseph answered and said, This is the interpretation thereof: The three baskets are three days: Yet within three days shall Pharaoh lift up thy head from off thee, and shall hang thee on a tree; and the birds shall eat thy flesh from off thee. And it came to pass the third day, which was Pharaoh's birthday, that he made a feast unto all his servants: and he lifted up the head of the chief butler and of the chief baker among his servants. And he restored the chief butler unto his butlership again; and he gave the cup into Pharaoh's hand: But he hanged the chief baker: as Joseph had interpreted to them. Yet did not the chief butler remember Joseph, but forgat him.

Now read through Genesis 41 for more insight.

And it came to pass at the end of two full years that Pharaoh dreamed: and, behold, he stood by the river. And, behold, there came up out of the river seven well favoured kine and fat-fleshed; and they fed in a meadow. And, behold, seven other kine came up after them out of the river, ill favoured and lean-fleshed; and stood by the other kine upon the brink of the river. And the ill favoured and lean-fleshed kine did eat up the seven well favoured and fat kine. So Pharaoh awoke. And he slept and dreamed the second time: and, behold, seven ears of corn came up upon one stalk, rank and good. And, behold, seven thin ears and blasted with the east wind sprung up after them. And the seven thin ears devoured the seven rank and full ears. And Pharaoh awoke, and, behold, it was a dream. And it came to pass in the morning that his spirit was troubled; and he sent and called for all the magicians of Egypt, and all the wise men thereof: and Pharaoh told them his dream; but there was none that could interpret them unto Pharaoh. Then spake the chief butler unto Pharaoh, saying, I do remember my faults this day: Pharaoh was wroth with his servants, and put me in ward in the captain of the guard's house, both me and the chief baker: And we dreamed a dream in one night, I and he; we dreamed each man according to the interpretation of his dream. And there was there with us a young man, an Hebrew, servant to the captain of the guard; and we told him, and he interpreted to us our dreams; to each man according to his dream he did interpret. And it came to pass, as he interpreted to us, so it was; me he restored unto mine office, and him he hanged. Then Pharaoh sent and called Joseph, and they brought him hastily out of the dungeon: and he shaved himself, and changed his raiment, and came in unto Pharaoh.

[15] And Pharaoh said unto Joseph, I have dreamed a dream, and there is none that can interpret it: and I have heard say of thee, that thou canst understand a dream to interpret it. And Joseph answered Pharaoh, saying, It is not in me: God shall give Pharaoh an answer of peace. And Pharaoh said unto Joseph, In my dream, behold, I stood upon the bank of the river: And, behold, there came up out of the river seven kine, fat-fleshed and well favoured; and they fed in a meadow: And, behold, seven other kine came up after them, poor and very ill favoured and lean-fleshed, such as I never saw in all the land of Egypt for badness: And the lean and the ill favoured kine

did eat up the first seven fat kine: And when they had eaten them up, it could not be known that they had eaten them; but they were still ill favoured, as at the beginning. So I awoke. And I saw in my dream, and, behold, seven ears came up in one stalk, full and good: And, behold, seven ears, withered, thin, and blasted with the east wind, sprung up after them: And the thin ears devoured the seven good ears: and I told this unto the magicians; but there was none that could declare it to me. And Joseph said unto Pharaoh, The dream of Pharaoh is one: God hath shewed Pharaoh what he is about to do. The seven good kine are seven years; and the seven good ears are seven years: the dream is one. And the seven thin and ill favoured kine that came up after them are seven years; and the seven empty ears blasted with the east wind shall be seven years of famine. This is the thing which I have spoken unto Pharaoh: What God is about to do he sheweth unto Pharaoh. Behold, there come seven years of great plenty throughout all the land of Egypt: And there shall arise after them seven years of famine; and all the plenty shall be forgotten in the land of Egypt; and the famine shall consume the land; And the plenty shall not be known in the land by reason of that famine following; for it shall be very grievous. And for that the dream was doubled unto Pharaoh twice; it is because the thing is established by God, and God will shortly bring it to pass. Now therefore let Pharaoh look out a man discreet and wise, and set him over the land of Egypt. Let Pharaoh do this, and let him appoint officers over the land, and take up the fifth part of the land of Egypt in the seven plenteous years. And let them gather all the food of those good years that come, and lay up corn under the hand of Pharaoh, and let them keep food in the cities. And that food shall be for store to the land against the seven years of famine, which shall be in the land of Egypt; that the land perish not through the famine. And the thing was good in the eyes of Pharaoh, and in the eyes of all his servants. And Pharaoh said unto his servants, Can we find such a one as this is, a man in whom the Spirit of God is? And Pharaoh said unto Joseph, Forasmuch as God hath shewed thee all this, there is none so discreet and wise as thou art: Thou shalt be over my house, and according unto thy word shall all my people be ruled: only in the throne will I be greater than thou. And Pharaoh said unto Joseph, See, I have set thee over all the land of Egypt. And Pharaoh took off his ring from his hand, and put it upon Joseph's hand, and arrayed him in vestures of fine linen, and put a gold chain about his neck; And he made him to ride in the second chariot which he had; and they cried before him, Bow the knee: and he made him ruler over all the land of Egypt. And Pharaoh said unto Joseph, I am Pharaoh, and without thee shall no man lift up his hand or foot in all the land of Egypt. And Pharaoh called Joseph's name Zaphnathpaaneah; and he gave him to wife Asenath the daughter of Potipherah priest of On. And Joseph went out over all the land of Egypt. And Joseph was thirty years old when he stood before Pharaoh king of Egypt. And Joseph went out from the presence of Pharaoh, and went throughout all the land of Egypt. And in the seven plenteous years the earth brought forth by handfuls. And he gathered up all the food of the seven years, which were in the land of Egypt, and laid up the food in the cities: the food of the field, which was round about every city, laid he up in the same. And Joseph gathered corn as the sand of the sea, very much, until he left numbering; for it was without number.

And unto Joseph were born two sons before the years of famine came, which Asenath the daughter of Potipherah priest of On bare unto him. And Joseph called the name of the firstborn Manasseh: For God, said he, hath made me forget all my toil, and all my father's house. And the name of the second called he Ephraim: For God hath caused me to be fruitful in the land of my affliction. And the seven years of plenteousness, that was in the land of Egypt, were ended. And the seven years of dearth began to come, according as Joseph had said: and the dearth was in all lands; but in all the land of Egypt there was bread. And when all the land of Egypt was famished, the people cried to Pharaoh for bread: and Pharaoh said unto all the Egyptians, Go unto Joseph; what he saith to you, do. And the famine was over all the face of the earth: and Joseph opened all the storehouses, and sold unto the Egyptians; and the famine waxed sore in the land of Egypt. And all countries came into Egypt to Joseph for to buy corn; because that the famine was so sore in all lands.

We see an eternal example of selfless service and how God started out by positioning things for the greatness of Joseph and for the great work that he did. Joseph was a slave in a strange land and a prisoner, but he did not allow any of these to stand in the way of what God was going to do. Twice, he stepped in to serve—firstly to interpret Pharaoh's dreams, which nobody else could, and secondly to take on the responsibility of ensuring that what God revealed through Pharoah's dreams were strictly followed because there was none better than he was in all the land of Egypt to understand how to go about such a divine service. Joseph could have begrudged Egypt, the land of his enslavement and unjustifiable imprisonment; however, he used his talents and gifts to serve these people selflessly for their good, and that was why God promoted him to the place of a god.

We can readily draw that conclusion from the name that Pharaoh gave to Joseph, Zaphnath-Paaneah, which probably means "God lives and He speaks" in the Egyptian language. There is nothing more revealing of the grace of God than the times when others begins to see God working, speaking, or shaping the world through man, and He can accomplish this through you, too. Through the oracle of selfless service, God's essence is revealed to you and all you serve, and that is doubly powerful.

True Worship

Real salvation is knowing and understanding the gift(s) of God in your life. Proverbs 18:, says, "A man's gift maketh room for him, and bringeth him before great men."

True worship and reaching a place of His presence—and I am using this reference more loosely—is an experience you can only achieve through the oracle of selfless service. Whether it is the giving of your resources for no apparent gain or of yourself for no foreseeable glory/fame at the cost of hard work, rejection, humiliation and failures or in prayer the seemingly powerless exercise at the cost of humility, weakness, painstaking self-denials and nightly watchings or the appropriating of God's goodness and promises for a people that does not deserve it. The oracle of selfless service is absolute form of surrendering all to His glory and being united with His divine purpose.

The oracle of selfless service is true worship that unites God's purpose with our daily living. God can reveal to your heart His plans for you, and you can make yourself available to work toward that plan's implementation. There is no better place with God Almighty, our Father. At the tomb of Lazarus, Jesus said the following in John 11:39–42:

> Jesus said, Take ye away the stone. Martha, the sister
> of him that was dead, saith unto him, Lord, by this time
> he stinketh: for he hath been dead four days. Jesus saith
> unto her, Said I not unto thee, that, if thou wouldest

believe, thou shouldest see the glory of God? Then they took away the stone from the place where the dead was laid. And Jesus lifted up his eyes, and said, Father, I thank thee that thou hast heard me. And I knew that thou hearest me always: but because of the people which stand by I said it, that they may believe that thou hast sent me.

In other words, He was saying that if you believed, you would see God's hand working through Him." And again thank you for hearing me, for I know that thou always hear me, but I am only saying this because of this people around here, so that they may believe that You have sent me. This is the only faith that leads to true salvation." – John 11: 42

Earlier on when He heard of the news of Lazarus sickness, He said this in John 11:4, "When Jesus heard that, he said, This sickness is not unto death, but for the glory of God, that the Son of God might be glorified thereby." He knew God the Father's plan to work in an unprecedented way so that the world could believe in the Son of God. This oracle is in you, not outside, not at the mercy of anybody. It is with you, and you can recognize and tap into it for the good of others and the world. You can see the glory of God practically flow through you. You can open blind eyes, feed the hungry, make believers out of skeptics, reach the lost and the religiously condemned, and most importantly, forge a living relationship with the Lord to help awaken the church of God and body of Christ worldwide and bring her to a greater prominence in this our generation.

Chapter 5

APPLICATION:
THE 21-DAYS PRAYER PROJECT

And such as do wickedly against the covenant shall
he corrupt by flatteries: but the people that do know
their God shall be strong, and do exploits.
—Daniel 11:32

Whenever a child of God is equipped with the Word of GOD (and the knowledge of God), fervent in prayer, and willing to step out in service of the Lord, the fullness of God is revealed in a new and incomprehensible way. Let us examine some accounts in the Bible that will help us in the application of these oracles of God in a personal way, the Holy Spirit helping us in our endeavor.

The Story of Rahab

Now consider Joshua 2.

> And Joshua the son of Nun sent out of Shittim two
> men to spy secretly, saying; Go view the land, even
> Jericho. And they went, and came into an harlot's house,
> named Rahab, and lodged there. And it was told the king

of Jericho, saying, Behold, there came men in hither to night of the children of Israel to search out the country. And the king of Jericho sent unto Rahab, saying, Bring forth the men that are come to thee, which are entered into thine house: for they be come to search out all the country. And the woman took the two men, and hid them, and said thus, There came men unto me, but I wist not whence they were: And it came to pass about the time of shutting of the gate, when it was dark, that the men went out: whither the men went I wot not: pursue after them quickly; for ye shall overtake them. But she had brought them up to the roof of the house, and hid them with the stalks of flax, which she had laid in order upon the roof. And the men pursued after them the way to Jordan unto the fords: and as soon as they which pursued after them were gone out, they shut the gate. And before they were laid down, she came up unto them upon the roof; And she said unto the men, I know that the LORD hath given you the land, and that your terror is fallen upon us, and that all the inhabitants of the land faint because of you. For we have heard how the LORD dried up the water of the Red sea for you, when ye came out of Egypt; and what ye did unto the two kings of the Amorites, that were on the other side Jordan, Sihon and Og, whom ye utterly destroyed. And as soon as we had heard these things, our hearts did melt, neither did there remain any more courage in any man, because of you: for the LORD your God, he is God in heaven above, and in earth beneath. Now therefore, I pray you, swear unto me by the LORD, since I have shewed you kindness, that ye will also shew kindness unto my father's house, and give me a true token: And that ye will save alive my father, and my mother, and my brethren, and my sisters, and all that they have, and deliver our lives from death.

And the men answered her, Our life for yours, if ye utter not this our business. And it shall be, when the LORD hath given us the land, that we will deal kindly and truly with thee. Then she let them down by a cord through the window: for her house was upon the town wall, and she dwelt upon the wall. And she said unto them, Get you to the mountain, lest the pursuers meet you; and hide yourselves there three days, until the pursuers be returned: and afterward may ye go your way. And the men said unto her, We will be blameless of this thine oath which thou hast made us swear. Behold, when we come into the land, thou shalt bind this line of scarlet thread in the window which thou didst let us down by: and thou shalt bring thy father, and thy mother, and thy brethren, and all thy father's household, home unto thee. And it shall be, that whosoever shall go out of the doors of thy house into the street, his blood shall be upon his head, and we will be guiltless: and whosoever shall be with thee in the house, his blood shall be on our head, if any hand be upon him. And if thou utter this our business, then we will be quit of thine oath which thou hast made us to swear. And she said, According unto your words, so be it. And she sent them away, and they departed: and she bound the scarlet line in the window. And they went, and came unto the mountain, and abode there three days, until the pursuers were returned: and the pursuers sought them throughout all the way, but found them not. So the two men returned, and descended from the mountain, and passed over, and came to Joshua the son of Nun, and told him all things that befell them: And they said unto Joshua, Truly the LORD hath delivered into our hands all the land; for even all the inhabitants of the country do faint because of us.

In this passage, we can deduce the power of knowing the will of God. Rahab knew what was about to happen just like everyone else in the city-state of Jericho. And she believed that the only way she could live and prosper was to fall into the hands of the Lord God and not fight against Him. The people of Jericho had heard of the acts of God in Egypt—the parting of the Red Sea and the destruction of the two kings on the other side of Jordan, Bashan king of Og and Sihon king of the Amorites, who tried to fight against the Israelites from coming through their land. Let us carefully consider her next line of action detailed in the Holy Scripture.

> And before they were laid down, she came up unto them upon the roof; And she said unto the men, I know that the LORD hath given you the land, and that your terror is fallen upon us, and that all the inhabitants of the land faint because of you. For we have heard how the LORD dried up the water of the Red sea for you, when ye came out of Egypt; and what ye did unto the two kings of the Amorites, that were on the other side Jordan, Sihon and Og, whom ye utterly destroyed. And as soon as we had heard these things, our hearts did melt, neither did there remain any more courage in any man, because of you: for the LORD your God, he is God in heaven above, and in earth beneath. Now therefore, I pray you, swear unto me by the LORD, since I have shewed you kindness, that ye will also shew kindness unto my father's house, and give me a true token: And that ye will save alive my father, and my mother, and my brethren, and my sisters, and all that they have, and deliver our lives from death. (Joshua 2:8–13)

With the limited knowledge of God she had, Rahab knew that the only way she could save herself and her family was to fall in line behind the people of God, who from all indications, were on the right side with God, and she knew that all who would stand against them were doomed for destruction. Not minding the risk, she decided to be an instrument in the hand of the Lord in saving the two spies. This is what the Bible says of her: "By faith the harlot Rahab perish not with them that believed not; when she had received the spies with peace" (Hebrews 11:31).

Here, faith in the acts of God, prayer, and the willingness to serve His purpose by helping God's people brought salvation to her and her father's house. The Lord continued to honor her long after that because the Messiah was given to us through her lineage.

David and Goliath

King David knew God personally. This was why God's Word was continually on his lips when we look at the following scriptures: "O how love I thy law! it is my meditation all the day" (Psalm 119:97). "How sweet are thy words unto my taste! Yea, sweeter than honey to my mouth" (Psalm 119:103). He was a man of prayer; most of his psalms were prayers. His willingness to do the will of God through the service of God's people was unprecedented. "And David said to Saul, Let no man's heart fail because of him; thy servant will go and fight with this Philistine" (1 Samuel 17:32).

In leading to the battle against Goliath, we can readily see King David invoke these three oracles of God, which were at his disposal. First of all, through his knowledge of God, he understood that the Lord was the Lord God of hosts, "the God of the armies of Israel." King David understood that God was the one that went before Israel in every battle they had ever fought. On the other hand, Goliath cursed David, "And the Philistine said unto David, Am I a dog, that thou comest to me with staves? And the Philistine cursed David by his gods. And the Philistine said to David, Come to me, and I will give thy flesh unto the fowls of the air, and to the beasts of the field" (1 Samuel 17: 43-44).

Goliath's confidence was in his stature, his weapons of war, and his undefeated streak. But King David was about to change all that as he declared to Goliath,

> Then said David to the Philistine, Thou comest to me with a sword, and with a spear, and with a shield: but I come to thee in the name of the LORD of hosts, the God of the armies of Israel, whom thou hast defied. This day will the LORD deliver thee into mine hand; and I will smite thee, and take thine head from thee; and I will give the carcases of the host of the Philistines this day unto the fowls of the air, and to the wild beasts of the earth; that all the earth may know that there is a God in Israel. And all this assembly shall know that the LORD saveth not with sword and spear: for the battle is the LORD's, and he will give you into our hands. (1 Samuel 17: 45-47).

David called God into the equation by invoking the oracle of prayer. We all know the rest. The story of David and Goliath has been well referenced by believers and unbelievers alike, as well as atheists throughout history because of the miraculous outcome. The destruction of Goliath is one vivid demonstration of these three constants in the Christian faith and how effective they have been as oracles through the ages in delivering the judgment of God.

Goliath could not stand against the boy David, who had only a sling and a stone but was an embodiment of these three oracles of GOD. He saw through the vain boast and threats of Goliath. There is a greater giant and a greater champion with better war strategy and weapons of warfare, and His name is the Lord God of hosts, whom the Philistine had defied by insulting the armies of Israel, whose head is the Lord. "And David spake to the men that stood by him, saying, What shall be done to the man that killeth this Philistine, and taketh away the reproach from Israel? for who is this uncircumcised Philistine, that he should defy the armies of the living God?" (1 Samuel 17:26).

Every believer possesses the right to be an embodiment of these oracles of God to wroth signs and wonders in this our dispensation. We can do so if we are willing to sacrifice our time and our resources to seek a personal knowledge of Him by becoming fervent in prayer and by cashing in on the opportunities that present themselves to serve others through Him and for Him.

The Contest at Mount Carmel

In the incident between Elijah and the prophets of Baal at Mount Carmel, one can observe so vividly these oracles at play.

> So Ahab sent unto all the children of Israel, and gathered the prophets together unto mount Carmel. And Elijah came unto all the people, and said, How long halt ye between two opinions? if the LORD be God, follow him: but if Baal, then follow him. And the people answered him not a word. Then said Elijah unto the people, I, even I only, remain a prophet of the LORD; but Baal's prophets are four hundred and fifty men. Let them therefore give us two bullocks; and let them choose one bullock for themselves, and cut it in pieces, and lay it on wood, and put no fire under: and I will dress the other bullock, and lay it on wood, and put no fire under: And call ye on the name of your gods, and I will call on the name of the LORD: and the God that answereth by fire, let him be God. And all the people answered and said, It is well spoken. And Elijah said unto the prophets of Baal, Choose you one bullock for yourselves, and dress it first; for ye are many; and call on the name of your gods, but put no fire under. And they took the bullock which was given them, and they dressed it, and called on the name

of Baal from morning even until noon, saying, O Baal, hear us. But there was no voice, nor any that answered. And they leaped upon the altar which was made. And it came to pass at noon, that Elijah mocked them, and said, Cry aloud: for he is a god; either he is talking, or he is pursuing, or he is in a journey, or peradventure he sleepeth, and must be awaked. And they cried aloud, and cut themselves after their manner with knives and lancets, till the blood gushed out upon them. And it came to pass, when midday was past, and they prophesied until the time of the offering of the evening sacrifice, that there was neither voice, nor any to answer, nor any that regarded. And Elijah said unto all the people, Come near unto me. And all the people came near unto him. And he repaired the altar of the LORD that was broken down. And Elijah took twelve stones, according to the number of the tribes of the sons of Jacob, unto whom the word of the LORD came, saying, Israel shall be thy name: And with the stones he built an altar in the name of the LORD: and he made a trench about the altar, as great as would contain two measures of seed. And he put the wood in order, and cut the bullock in pieces, and laid him on the wood, and said, Fill four barrels with water, and pour it on the burnt sacrifice, and on the wood. And he said, Do it the second time. And they did it the second time. And he said, Do it the third time. And they did it the third time. And the water ran round about the altar; and he filled the trench also with water. And it came to pass at the time of the offering of the evening sacrifice, that Elijah the prophet came near, and said, LORD God of Abraham, Isaac, and of Israel, let it be known this day that thou art God in Israel, and that I am thy servant, and that I have done all these things at thy word. Hear me,

O LORD, hear me, that this people may know that thou art the LORD God, and that thou hast turned their heart back again. Then the fire of the LORD fell, and consumed the burnt sacrifice, and the wood, and the stones, and the dust, and licked up the water that was in the trench. And when all the people saw it, they fell on their faces: and they said, The LORD, he is the God; the LORD, he is the God. And Elijah said unto them, Take the prophets of Baal; let not one of them escape. And they took them: and Elijah brought them down to the brook Kishon, and slew them there. (1 Kings 18:20–40)

From this passage, we can see Elijah armed with the Word of God and the knowledge of Him. He first repaired the altar of the Lord, according to biblical standards. "And there shall thou build an altar unto the LORD thy GOD, an altar of stones: thou shall not lift up any iron tool upon them. Thou shall build the altar of the LORD thy GOD of whole stones: and thou shall offer burnt offerings thereon unto the LORD thy GOD" (Deuteronomy 27:5–6)

And then he prayed, "And it came to pass at the time of the offering of the evening sacrifice, that Elijah the prophet came near, and said, LORD God of Abraham, Isaac, and of Israel, let it be known this day that thou art God in Israel, and that I am thy servant, and that I have done all these things at thy word. Hear me, O LORD, hear me, that this people may know that thou art the LORD God, and that thou hast turned their heart back again" (1 Kings 18:36–7).

But in all these, he was motivated by service. He wanted to prove to the northern kingdom that Baal was not God and that they needed to turn their hearts back to the God of Israel that brought them out of the bondage of Egypt and gave them the land of Canaan—a land flowing with milk and honey. Elijah called for the contest against the prophets of Baal at Mount Carmel, when he challenged them by saying: "the GOD that answereth by fire let him be GOD."

> Then the fire of the LORD fell, and consumed the
> burnt sacrifice, and the wood, and the stones, and the
> dust, and licked up the water that was in the trench.
> And when all the people saw it, they fell on their faces:
> and they said, The LORD, he is the God; the LORD, he is
> the God. And Elijah said unto them, Take the prophets
> of Baal; let not one of them escape. And they took them:
> and Elijah brought them down to the brook Kishon, and
> slew them there. (1 Kings 18:38–40).

In this contest at Mount Carmel, the raw power of God was demonstrated before the eyes of all who were there. A single man discounted the lies of the worshipers of Baal and their popular beliefs of the day. Their rituals of enchantments, dancing, and cutting themselves for blood proved futile, and these were of no match to the man of God, not with Elijah's prayers and willingness to do the will of God selflessly.

For the fire to fall from heaven, the prophet Elijah had to apply his knowledge of God (the oracle of God's Word) in repairing the altar. He had to actually pray and call upon the Lord God Almighty, who is the consuming fire (the oracle of prayer). He was motivated to do whatever it took to reveal the God of Israel as the Almighty God and no other and to help turn the hearts of the children of Israel to their maker and helper (the oracle of selfless service). These oracles still work the same wonders today, and the people of God should take advantage of them. The Lord is waiting to pour out His revival fire upon us. Just make the move. This book is a holy cry for believers to revive these oracles of God, a call that if heeded will stir up personal revival and throughout the Church of God. This is why I am recommending that you do the 21- days prayer project, which I have provided in the following pages. These prayers will get you started with your prayer life, help you learn and master the arts of praying, as well as prove God's faithfulness to you personally. There are seven sections of three days each that must be prayed consecutively. I also recommend that you do some form of fasting if you can, but if you have any medical issues you may want to consult your doctor, before you engage in any form of fast. Pray at the midnight hour for the most effective results. Furthermore, if the followimg set of prayers points seem strange to you, read this; "And Jesus answering saith unto them. Have faith in God. For verily I say unto you. That whosoever shall say unto this mountain, Be thou removed, and be cast into the sea; and shall not doubt in his heart, but shall believe that those things he saith shall come to pass; he shall have whatsoever he saith. Therefore I say unto you, what things soever ye desire when ye pray, believe that ye have receive them and ye shall have them." –Mark 11:22-24. Your mountains are the things these prayer points address. Note also what the bible says in the book of Job 22:28 "Thou shalt also decree a thing, an it shall be established unto thee: and the light shall shine in thy ways." The Lord meet you at the point of your needs, in Jesus' name. Amen!

I recommend that you read through the entire book of Jeremiah during your 21-days prayer project. Start your prayer everyday by reading Isaiah 49, daily and confess out loud the scriptural confessions following. Then begin singing songs of praise and worship for at least 20 minutes. Remember to do these for the entire 21-days. Thereafter, take the prayer points boldly, spend 2 to 3 minutes on each prayer point. Pray standing and pray out loud.

21-Days Prayer Project

Day One through Three
Twenty-One-Day Prayer and Fasting Program

Scriptural Reading: Isaiah 49
Confessions: Isaiah 8:9–10 and Revelation: 3:7–9

1. Confess all your sin before the Lord God Almighty. Ask the Holy Ghost to convict and bring to remembrance every sin in your life that you have not yet confessed. Confess the sin of your parents and grandparents. Begin to repent for every sin that you have confessed in your life and your generations passed. Ask the Lord for mercy and receive forgiveness from His hands. Now begin to plead (ask for) the blood of Jesus against every sin you have confessed and repent from them. Ask the blood of Jesus to wash you, purge you, and cleanse you from every sin and their stains upon your life.

Praise and Worship

Sing songs of praise for at least twenty minutes each day.

Prayer Points

1. Oh, Lord, by your power terminate every evil progress in my life, in the mighty name of Jesus.

2. Let every root of sin in my life dry up by the fire of the Holy Ghost, in Jesus' name.

3. Every sin programmed into my genes be cut off by the sword of the spirit, in the name of Jesus.

4. Blood of Jesus, separate me from any idolatrous ancestry, in the name of Jesus.

5. I denounce and renounce every conscious and unconscious evil covenant I have entered into, in Jesus' name.

6. I am in Christ. I am a new creation. Old things are passed away. Behold, everything is become new. Let the old man in me disappear and let the new man appear, in Jesus' name.

7. I detach myself from every ancestral covenant, in the name of Jesus.

8. Every parental curse over my life be broken today by the blood of Jesus, in the name of Jesus.

9. Every curse of my native land operating in my life be broken now, in Jesus' name.

10. Every curse of past sexual partners in my life be broken now, in Jesus' name.

11. Every curse because of sin in my life be broken now, in Jesus' name.

12. Let every attachment to familiar spirit in my life be severed, in the name of Jesus.

13. I reject every spell of witchcraft upon my life, in the mighty name of Jesus.

14. By my position in Christ Jesus, in heavenly places, I dethrone principalities, powers, dominions, and spiritual wickedness in high places, in Jesus' name.

15. God of Abraham, Isaac, and Jacob, arise and deliver me from my oppressors, in the mighty name of Jesus.

16. Holy Spirit of God, help thou my infirmities, in the name of Jesus.

17. Oh, Lord, by your power by which you divided the Red Sea, bring me from where I am to where you want me to be, in Jesus' name.

18. Every human agent incensed against my destiny, destroy yourselves, in the mighty name of Jesus.

19. Every battle for my soul by the kingdom of darkness, be overthrown, in Jesus' name.

20. Let every attack that has derailed my destiny be overturn, overturn, and overturn, in the name of Jesus.

21. Oh, Lord my Father, cause my destroyers and my wasters to go away from me, in the name of Jesus.

22. O thou balm of Gilead, heal my spiritual wounds, in the mighty name of Jesus.

23. I shall not die but live to declare the praise of my God, in Jesus' name.

24. Oh, Lord, my God, deliver me from the mire and let me not sink, let me be delivered from them that hate me and out of the deep waters, in Jesus' name.

25. They gave me gall for my meat, and in my thirst, they gave me vinegar to drink. Let their table become a snare before them, and that which should have been for their welfare, let it become a trap, in Jesus' name.

26. Pour out thine indignation upon them, and let your wrathful anger take hold of those that hate me, oh, Lord, in Jesus' name.

27. And behold at evening tide trouble, and before the morning, he is not. And this is the portion of them that spoil us, and the lot of those that rob us, in the name of Jesus.

28. Let all those who seek the Lord rejoice and be glad in thee, and let such as love thy salvation say continually. Let God be magnified, in Jesus' name.

29. Every external evil aggression against my life, ministry, health, and finances, be rendered null and void, in the mighty name of Jesus.

30. Let every witchcraft conspiracy against my life be overturned, overturned, and overturned, in the name of Jesus.

31. Oh, Lord, God of Abraham, Isaac, and Israel, invoke the ten plagues of Egypt against my stubborn enemies, in Jesus' name.

32. Every evil expectation against my destiny be frustrated, in the name of Jesus.

33. Let every chronic problem keeping me from doing exploits for God be arrested and be overturned, overturned, and overturned, in Jesus' name.

34. I command every evil emitting contrary energy against my destiny to explode and be totally destroyed, in the name of Jesus.

35. Let they who are adversaries to my soul be confounded and be consumed. Let they who seek my hurt be covered with reproach and dishonor, in Jesus' name.

36. Oh, thou great physician, by the power for which you are known to be God, heal me from every chronic disease, in Jesus' name.

37. Oh, Lord, other lords beside thee have had dominion over us, but by thee only, we will make mention of your name, in Jesus' name.

38. Blood of Jesus, silence every voice speaking fear, defeat, and worthlessness into my life and speak better things over me, in the name of Jesus.

39. Let the path of those who are after my soul be dark and slippery, and let the angels of the Lord pursue them, in the name of Jesus.

40. Let the curse of the bread of affliction and bitter water over my life be broken now, in Jesus' name.

41. Because they love cursing, so let it come upon them, and because they love not blessing, let it be far from them. This shall be the portion of those who curse me, in the name of Jesus.

42. I frustrate every attempt to keep my eagle down, for my eagle must soar to great heights, in the name of Jesus.

43. Oh, Lord, revoke every evil covenant from my place of birth and anywhere I have called home, in the name of Jesus.

44. I call fire from heaven against every spirit of Sanballat and Tobiah, mocking my destiny, in Jesus' name.

45. Every giant enemy before me, receive the stones of fire, in the name of Jesus.

46. Every evil association for my sake, scatter now and be broken into irreparable pieces, in Jesus' name.

47. Pray for Persecuted Christians all over the world for at least 5 minutes, in Jesus' name.

48. Pray for the nation of Israel for at least 5 minutes, in Jesus' name.

49. Prayer for the baptism of the Holy Ghost and fire for at least 15 minutes, in Jesus' name.

Days Four through Six
Twenty-One-Day Prayer and Fasting Program

Scriptural Reading: Isaiah 49
Confessions: Isaiah 8:9–10 and Revelation: 3:7–9.

Praise and Worship:

Sing songs of praise for at least twenty minutes.

Prayer Points

1. Every last battle before me this year, I turn you over unto the Lord God Almighty, in Jesus's name.

2. Every organized network of human agents and spirits against my destiny, turn against yourself, in the mighty name of Jesus.

3. Father Lord, turn over the honor of my adversaries to me and my shame to the enemies of my soul, in the name of Jesus.

4. I will not go to the gallows. My enemy shall go on my behalf, in the mighty name of Jesus.

5. Let every health condition in my life that has defied medicine receive the touch of the most high, in Jesus' name.

6. Let the accusers of my life be found liars and let them be silenced forever, in the name of Jesus.

7. Every arrow of the enemy in my life begin to jump out now, in Jesus' name.

8. Oh, Lord, turn the trusted counsel of the wicked against my life to foolishness, in the mighty name of Jesus.

9. Every spiritual exchange of my body parts and organs be recovered and be restored to me, in Jesus' name.

10. Every witchcraft disease planted into my body, I command you to come out of me and go back to your sender, in Jesus' name.

11. Oh, Lord, give me strength in my fainting and increase my strength where I have no might, in the name of Jesus.

12. Father Lord, as I wait upon you, renew my strength, cause me to mount up with wings as eagles, let me run and not be weary and walk and not faint, in Jesus' name.

13. The Lord is on my side, I will not fear, what man can do to me, in the name of Jesus.

14. Help me, O, Lord, my God, O, save me according to thy mercy, in Jesus' name.

15. Let my adversaries be clothed with shame, and let them cover themselves with their confusion, as with a mantle, in the mighty name of Jesus.

16. My body is the temple of the most high. He will not share me with any disease. Therefore, sicknesses and diseases, jump out now, in the name of Jesus.

17. Oh, Lord, give me victory in the battle that will bring me to renown, in the name of Jesus.

18. Every owner of evil load in my life, I summon you now. Come and carry your load, in the name of Jesus.

19. Every prince of wickedness positioned in the heavenlies to detain and divert my blessings. Receive brimstone, sulfur, and unquenchable fire, in the name of Jesus.

20. All my blessings that have been stolen spiritually in the dreams, be restored now, in the name of Jesus.

21. Oh, God of Abraham, Isaac, and Jacob, remove from me every limit set over my life by the Enemy, in Jesus' name.

22. Every deception to rob me of my birthright be overturn, overturn, and overturn, in the mighty name of Jesus.

23. Oh, Lord, vindicate me from every wicked condemnation, in the mighty name of Jesus.

24. Father Lord, grant me good health, long life, and prosperity, in the name of Jesus.

25. Every attempt to keep me from my God-given destiny be overturn, overturn, and overturn, in the mighty name of Jesus.

26. Let the waters of every marine witchcraft incensed against my destiny dry up and let fire fall from heaven and consume them, in the name of Jesus.

27. Oh, Lord, deliver me from every spirit spouse, in the name of Jesus.

28. Every power spirit or personalities that violate me in the dream receive the judgment of the Lord and be cast into the lake of fire, in Jesus' name.

29. Every dream oppressor working against my peace and prosperity be destroyed now, in the name of Jesus.

30. Oh, Lord, do not pull back your sword until the last enemy of my soul is cut down, in the name of Jesus.

31. Oh, Lord, give me a gift that will make me a sort after, in the name of Jesus.

32. Oh, Lord, mandate your angels to search the bottom of waters, under the earth, and the heavens to recover and restore all my stolen blessings, in the name of Jesus.

33. I will not let you go unless you bless me Lord, in the name of Jesus.

34. Pray for persecuted Christians all over the world for at least five minutes.

35. Pray for the nation of Israel for at least five minutes.

36. Pray for the baptism of the Holy Ghost and fire for at least ten minutes.

Days Seven through Nine
Twenty-One-Day Prayer and Fasting Program

Scriptural Reading: Isaiah 49
Confessions: Isaiah 8:9–10 and Revelation: 3:7–9

Praise and Worship:

Sing songs of praise for at least twenty minutes.

Prayer Points

1. Every familiar spirits of my father's house and my compound holding me hostage, receive brimstone, sulfur, and unquenchable fire, in the name of Jesus

2. Every conscious and unconscious initiation into witchcraft in my life, be exposed and be consumed by fire, in Jesus' name.

3. I challenge my body gates with the blood of Jesus and the fire of the Holy Ghost, in the mighty name of Jesus.

4. Let every organ in my body responding to witchcraft command (spells), receive deliverance now, in Jesus' name.

5. By the authority in the name of Jesus, by the power in the blood of Jesus and by the anointing of the Holy Ghost, let the yoke of every idol, altar, and ancestral covenant in my life be broken, in Jesus' name.

6. Evil yokes of unfriendly friends upon my life be broken, in the mighty name of Jesus.

7. Every ground operations in my hometown against my destiny, scatter and be utterly destroyed, in the name of Jesus.

8. Father Lord, break the wings of every flying power operating against my life, in Jesus' name.

9. Every spiritual poison in my life through food, drink, or sex, come out now, in the mighty name of Jesus.

10. Every silent pier competition and jealousy against my destiny, be undone by the blood of Jesus.

11. Every star destroyer from my hometown caging my star and my destiny, destroy yourselves, in the name of Jesus.

12. Jehovah Sabboath, deliver my star from the spirits of Pharaoh and Herod, in the mighty name of Jesus.

13. Oh, Lord, remove me from the list of those with wasted and unfulfilled destiny, in Jesus' name.

14. Every power that has mortgaged their destiny in order to destroy mine, my destiny is not your candidate. Be visited by the terror of the Most High God and perish, in the mighty name of Jesus.

15. Oh, thou that called forth Lazarus from the grave, call out my buried destiny, in the name of Jesus.

16. Any power, spirit, or personality using my personal belongings to manipulate my life, receive an angelic slap and be stricken with lightening, in the mighty name of Jesus.

17. Oh, Lord, my Father, deliver me from every evil in my life. Recover and restore all my stolen blessings because of the activities of manipulators, in Jesus' name.

18. Let the favor of the Lord God Almighty wash over me, and let the disappointments and rejections of the past disappear, in Jesus' name.

19. O, thou that has the key of David, grant unto me an open door to my divine blessings and shut the doors of evil permanently in my life, in Jesus' name.

20. O, thou that deliver Daniel from the lion den, deliver me from every eminent disaster today, in the name of Jesus.

21. O, thou fourth man in the fire, command the fire around me to lose its burning power, in the name of Jesus.

22. Every spell of the dust operating against my life, be undone in the name of Jesus.

23. Every jinx/padlock operating against my destiny be broken now, in Jesus' name.

24. Every bondage of idols and evil alters of my father's house and my native land, be destroyed by the blood of Jesus, in Jesus' name.

25. Every bewitchment operating against my life, be utterly destroyed by the blood of Jesus, in the mighty name of Jesus.

26. I look unto you, oh, Lord, for deliverance, do not leave me at the mercy of the destroyers, in the name of Jesus.

27. Let every satanic storm gathering against me, hear the voice of the Most High and disperse now, in Jesus' name.

28. Wherever any rituals or sacrifice has been performed in my name and against me, let thunder from the Lord strike and destroy everyone concern, the idol, the altar, and the priest, in Jesus' name.

29. I renounce and denounce every blood sacrifice performed for my sake, in the name of Jesus.

30. Let the evil day come upon those who have refused to let me go, in the name of Jesus.

31. Every occupant of my place in destiny, be thrown down now by thunder, in the name of Jesus.

32. Oh, Lord, help me to finish this year on a positive balance sheet in my health, finances, ministry, business, etc., in the name of Jesus.

33. I will not give up because my God has not given up on me, in Jesus' name.

34. I summon to battle every power, spirit, and personality laying claim to my destiny, in the name of Jesus.

35. I call for war of fire between me and my full-time enemies, in the mighty name of Jesus.

36. Pray for persecuted Christians all over the world for at least five minutes

37. Pray for the nation of Israel for at least five minutes.

38. Pray for the baptism of the Holy Ghost for at least ten minutes.

Days Ten through Twelve
Twenty-One-Day Prayer and Fasting Program

Scriptural Reading: Isaiah 49
Confessions: Isaiah 8:9–10 and Revelation: 3:7–9

Praise and Worship:

Sing songs of praise for at least twenty minutes.

Prayer Points

1. I challenge every permanent evil in my life, with the blood of Jesus Christ of Nazareth, in Jesus' name.

2. Let the root of every sickness and disease in my life be cut off with the sword of fire, in the mighty name of Jesus.

3. Oh, Lord, bless me indeed. Enlarge and establish my territories for me to shatter the limit of poverty, in Jesus' name.

4. I shall not borrow but lend to nations. Therefore, every curse of debt operating against my destiny be revoked now, by the power in the blood of Jesus, in the mighty name of Jesus.

5. I shall be the head and not the tail. I shall be above only and not beneath. Therefore, every yoke of the tail and beneath upon my life, be destroyed in the mighty name of Jesus.

6. Every snare of the fowler and trap of the enemy keeping me from the good things of life, release me and catch your owners now, in Jesus' name.

7. Let the bondage of blessings running out just before my turn be broken from my life, in the mighty name of Jesus.

8. Let every chronic failures, defeat, loss, and meaningless dream in my life be terminated by the anointing of the Holy Ghost, in the name of Jesus.

9. Every hired Balaam cursing my destiny, fall backward, break your neck, and perish, in the mighty name of Jesus.

10. Holy Ghost, help me to reject every masked invitation to sin in my life, in the name of Jesus.

11. Let every permanent spiritual stagnancy in my life be terminated by the Holy Ghost fire, in Jesus' name.

12. Oh, Lord, grant me four portions of the anointing of Elisha, in the mighty name of Jesus.

13. I will not be diverted or distracted at the point of my breakthrough, in the name of Jesus.

14. Oh, earth, oh, earth, oh, earth, open up and swallow every evil opposition determined to frustrate my destiny, in the name of Jesus.

15. Every water spirit demanding my worship, get thee behind me, in the mighty name of Jesus.

16. Oh, Lord, I open up my life unto your kingdom. Let me experience the greatness, power, glory, victory, and majesty of heaven for one day, in the name of Jesus.

17. Thy kingdom come, thy will be done on earth and in my life today, in the mighty name of Jesus.

18. Every power assigned to arrest me, be stricken with blindness and stagger to your destruction, in the name of Jesus.

19. The sun shall not smite me by day, nor the moon by night, in Jesus' name.

20. Lord Jesus, by your resurrection power, let every dead and dying good thing in my life come alive now, in Jesus mighty name.

21. I release the blood of Jesus against every evil operation of the enemy in my life, in Jesus' name.

22. Oh, Lord, release your angels to cast down the agents of sin assigned against my life, in the mighty name of Jesus.

23. Let every persistence evil in my life because of satanic gang-ups against me in the past be terminated, in the name of Jesus.

24. Every evil associated with my family name be terminated for my sake, in Jesus' name.

25. By the precious blood of Jesus, I claim the blessings of Abraham, and I reject the curses in my natural lineage, in Jesus' name.

26. Oh, Lord, equip me with anointing of the Holy Ghost, fire, and the blood of Jesus as I take the battle to the gates of the enemy, in the name of Jesus.

27. I will not be by passed over by my angel of blessing, and my helpers will not miss me, in Jesus' name.

28. Whatever blessings the Lord God Almighty has released for me, be loosed from witchcraft captivity, in the name of Jesus.

29. I bind the strong man of my father's house, my compound, and my native land, and I take away their spoils, in Jesus' name.

30. Lord Jesus, have compassion on me, lift me up from my low estate as you pass by me today, in the name of Jesus.

31. The enemies that trample me under their feet shall also worship before my feet, in the name of Jesus.

32. Pray for the persecuted Christian all over the world for at least five minutes.

33. Pray for the nation of Israel for at least five minutes.

34. Pray for the baptism of the Holy Ghost and fire for at least ten minutes.

Days Thirteen through Fifteen
Twenty-One-Day Prayer and Fasting Program

Scriptural Reading: Isaiah 49
Confessions: Isaiah 8:9–10 and Revelation: 3:7–9

Praise and Worship:

Sing songs of praise for at least twenty minutes.

Prayer Points

1. I release the blood of Jesus upon my environment, against every satanic stronghold, strongman, and evil throne assigned to dominate my destiny, in Jesus' name.

2. Let every ritual and sacrifice causing demonic trafficking in and out of my environment be doomed, in the mighty name of Jesus.

3. Every witchcraft activity in my environment be visited by the thunder fire of God and perish, in the name of Jesus.

4. Every local power strategically positioned in my environment to swallow the prayer of Christians and to frustrate the gospel of our Lord and Savior, I command you to flee or you perish, in the name of Jesus.

5. Holy Ghost, enthrone Jesus Christ of Nazareth in my environment and let every force of darkness collapse and perish, in Jesus' name.

6. Evil arrows flying around my environment shall not locate me and my household, in the mighty name of Jesus.

7. Every evil ground operation in my environment be frustrated and be terminated, in Jesus' name.

8. Evil landmarks serving as rallying points for demons and evil spirit in my environment be desolated, in the mighty name of Jesus.

9. I bind every spiritual robber in my environment with fetters of fire, and I spoil them, in Jesus' name.

10. Let every religious human agents representing any idol in my environment, be confused and be confounded, in the mighty name of Jesus.

11. I shall not be drowned out by the forces of evil in my environment. I shall shine as a light on a hilltop, in Jesus' name.

12. I refuse to be corrupted by the evil of the day. Oh, Lord, use me to turn men unto you, in the name of Jesus.

13. It is written: Our weapons of warfare are not canal but mighty through God to the pulling down of strongholds;. Therefore, I pull down evil strongholds in my environment by fire, in the mighty name of Jesus.

14. Every wickedness directed against me, return to your source, in the mighty name of Jesus.

15. Let every religious ritual to cause me to slumber and to manipulate me in the dream be frustrated, in the mighty name of Jesus.

16. Every environmental prince holding my blessings hostage, I call for angelic reinforcement against you and command you to release my blessing, in the name of Jesus Christ.

17. I shall not be a victim of the environment. My household shall not be a victim of the environment. We shall prevail over our environment, in Jesus' name.

18. Oh, Lord God, for my sake, let the curse of brassy heaven and iron ground my environment be broken. Open my heaven, oh, Lord, and bless my land, in the name of Jesus.

19. Let every curse of backwardness in my life be broken. Let progress begin to abound in my life and newness overtake old things in my life, in the name of Jesus.

20. It is written: Behold, I have received commandment to bless, and he hath blessed. And I cannot reverse it. These shall be the words of the evil powers hired to curse me, in the name of Jesus.

21. Oh, Lord, my Father, walk back every wicked spiritual and physical aggression against my finances, ministry, health, etc., in Jesus' name.

22. I take to the Lord God Almighty every battle of the accuser and the wasters raging against me, in the mighty name of Jesus.

23. Let every warfare of the emptiers and wasters against my destiny be terminated now, in Jesus' name.

24. It is written: They fought from heaven; the stars in their courses fought against Sisera; oh Lord, empower me to fight from heaven and the stars in their courses against the enemies of my soul, in Jesus' name.

25. It is written: He that leadeth in captivity shall go into captivity; he that killeth with the sword shall be killed with the sword, this is the patience and the faith of the saints (Revelation 13: 10); based upon this eternal word of God; I lead my captivity captive, and I destroy my destroyers, in Jesus' name.

26. My dry bones shall rise again, no matter what the enemies of my soul do, in Jesus' name.

27. Oh, thou who turns dry grounds into pool of waters and the wilderness into a highway, visit me today, in the name of Jesus.

28. Pray for the persecuted Christians all over the world for at least five minutes.

29. Pray for the nations of Israel for at least five minutes.

30. Pray for the baptism of the Holy Ghost and fire for at least ten minutes.

Days Sixteen through eighteen
Twenty-One-Day Prayer and Fasting Program

Scriptural Reading: Isaiah 49
Confessions: Isaiah 8:9–10 and Revelation: 3:7–9

Praise and Worship:

Sing songs of praise for at least twenty minutes.

Prayer Points

1. It is written: And I will give unto thee the keys of the kingdom of heaven, and whatsoever thou shalt bound on earth shall be bind in heaven: and whatsoever thou shalt loose on earth shall be loosed in heaven (MattHew 16:19): based upon this eternal word of God; Lord Jesus give unto me the keys of the kingdom of heaven to bind the powers of darkness and to lose my blessings in captivity, in the name of Jesus.

2. Oh, Lord, give me power to tread on serpents and scorpions and all the works of the enemies and let nothing hurt me, in the mighty name of Jesus.

3. Let every door of darkness keeping me from the light of God's presence be bulldozed by the earthquake of the Lord, in Jesus' name.

4. Oh, Lord, my Father, release the terror of the four lepers against every wicked siege before me, in the mighty name of Jesus.

5. Thou God of breakthroughs, break forth against the limits of poverty and debt in my life after the order of Baal-perazin (2 Samuel 5: 20), in Jesus' name.

6. Father Lord, give me the power to pass through the waters without them overflowing me and the fire without being burnt, in the name of Jesus.

7. Hold no more thy peace, oh, Lord. Rise up for me and promote me to the place of honor, in Jesus' name.

8. Father, reduce to naught every threat of the wicked and cause to perish every boastings of the enemy against my destiny, in the mighty name of Jesus.

9. Every power basking in my glory, be poured out and be brought down to the ground, in the mighty name of Jesus.

10. I recall every warfare that I have ever lost, holding my destiny hostage, and I fight back with the blood of Jesus and the fire of the Holy Ghost to recover my destiny, in Jesus' name.

11. Oh, Lord, fight for me every financial battle I have lost in the past and give me victory, in the name of Jesus.

12. Let those gloating over my past defeat beware. My God has heard my cry and shall arise to avenge me, in the name of Jesus.

13. Let every pursuit to cut me off from my Promised Land be drowned and perish, in the name of Jesus.

14. Every strongman assigned to watch my rising, fall into a deep sleep, and every mountain of obstacle before me, be removed from my path by the angels of the Lord, in Jesus' name.

15. Let the rejoicing of the enemies against me turn to weeping in the next few days, in the mighty name of Jesus.

16. Oh, Lord, my God, command an end to all my sufferings, in the name of Jesus.

17. It is written: One of you shall chase one thousand and two shall put them ten thousand to flight: I receive the keys of the kingdom of heaven, to put one thousand to flight and cause my enemies to flee before me, in Jesus' name.

18. Oh, Lord, turn my night into day and my failure to success for your name sake, in the name of Jesus.

19. It is written: It is the Lord's mercy that we are not consumed, because His compassion fail not; based upon this eternal word of God; because of thy mercies' oh Lord we shall not be consumed and for thy compassion that fail not, in Jesus' name.

20. It is written: All nations compassed me about, but in the name of the Lord, I destroy them, based upon this eternal word of God; I destroy every nation that has compassed me about, in the name of Jesus Christ of Nazareth.

21. My Lord and my Father give me an eleventh hour miracle this year, in the mighty name of Jesus.

22. Father Lord, feed the enemies of my soul with their own flesh and let them be drunken with their own blood, in Jesus' name.

23. Oh, Lord, contend with those who contend against me and show them you are my redeemer and my Savior, in the mighty name of Jesus.

24. Every carryover of any evil into the new year in my life, be terminated in the name of Jesus.

25. Every good thing yet to manifest in my life this year, I command you to appear now, in Jesus' name.

26. My Father, give me a testimony that will make people ask,

"How did that happen?" and to say, "Take me to your God," in Jesus mighty name.

27. Let every seasonal routine of evil in my life be terminated, in the mighty name of Jesus.

28. Pray for the persecuted Christians all over the world for at least five minutes.

29. Pray for the nations of Israel for at least five minutes.

30. Pray for the baptism of the Holy Ghost and fire for at least ten minutes.

Days Nineteen through Twenty-One
Twenty-One-Day Prayer and Fasting Program

Scriptural Reading: Isaiah 49
Confessions: Isaiah 8:9–10 and Revelation: 3:7–9

Praise and Worship:

Sing songs of praise for at least twenty minutes.

Prayer Points

1. O, Lord God Almighty, be thou my defense and cause me to prosper, in the name of Jesus.

2. Let every seed of poverty in my genes be replace by the blood Jesus, in Jesus' name

3. Dear Lord, my heavenly Father, bless me despite any ancestral covenant with poverty in my foundation, in the mighty name of Jesus.

4. Oh, Lord, my God, forgive me of every sin at the root of poverty in my life and family, in Jesus' name.

5. Let every curse at the core of poverty in my life and family be broken for my sake, in the mighty name of Jesus.

6. I draw the bloodline of Jesus against the spirits of debts and poverty in my life. Let them never cross paths with me anymore, in Jesus' name.

7. Blood of Jesus, wash away every trouble of the past from my finances. Let them not resurface or influence me anymore from today, in the name of Jesus.

8. Oh, Lord, my Father, bless me with a blessing that cannot be duplicated or insulted, in the name of Jesus.

9. I muster every power, given to me by the Lord God Almighty, to exhume my buried destiny and to cause the eagle in me to mount up with wings, in the name of Jesus.

10. Every spiritual wall of Jericho at the gate of my blessing, fall down flat, in the mighty name of Jesus.

11. Oh, Lord, my heavenly Father, move the ends of the world for me, in the name of Jesus.

12. Let those I have never known and have never met go out of their way to favor me and to bless me, in Jesus' name.

13. Bless the Lord, O my soul for all His benefits toward me, in the mighty name of Jesus.

14. Let the sun of this year stand still until you have avenged the enemies of my destiny and recovered all my blessings that were once taken hostage, in Jesus' name.

15. Let every wicked verdict against my life be reversed today by the precious blood of Jesus, in Jesus' name.

16. Let every evil nail fastened in their sure places be removed and be cut down and fall, and the burden that is upon it be cut off for my sake, in the mighty name of Jesus.

17. Let the appearance of my victory spell doom to every power there be celebrated for my past failures, in the name of Jesus.

18. You evil waters of my native land, release my blessings in your depths and possessions, in Jesus' name.

19. Let my blood become poison in the stomach of the drinker's

blood and draw thunder and earthquakes upon evil altars where it is offered, in the mighty name of Jesus.

20. I receive commandments to prosper. I shall not be poor. I receive commandments to lend to many nations. I shall not borrow, in Jesus' name.

21. Pray for the persecuted Christians all over the world for at least five minutes.

22. Pray for the nations of Israel for at least five minutes.

23. Pray for the baptism of the Holy Ghost and fire for at least ten minutes.

24. Praise the Lord who answers prayers.